POETIC

Spiritual

INSIGHT

POETIC
Spiritual
INSIGHT

BEATRICE E. GOETZ

WINEPRESS **WP** PUBLISHING

© 2003 by Beatrice E. Goetz. All rights reserved.

Printed in the United States of America.

Cover by Ragont Design.

Packaged by WinePress Publishing, PO Box 428, Enumclaw, WA 98022. The views expressed or implied in this work do not necessarily reflect those of WinePress Publishing. The author is ultimately responsible for the design, content, and editorial accuracy of this work.

Unless otherwise noted all Scriptures are taken from the King James Version of the Bible.

ISBN 1-57921-452-5
Library of Congress Catalog Card Number: 2002101088

Dedication

I dedicate this book to my husband Ray, my lifelong partner, and to our six children—Gary, Diane, Deborah, Thomas, John, and James—and their spouses, who have brought me much joy and happiness during my lifetime. I also want to give God the glory due Him for sending us eighteen grandchildren and four great-grandchildren, the first of whom Jesus called to His arms at the age of three months and twenty-four days.

The Bible

Within that awful volume lies
The mysteries of mysteries.
Happiness they of human race . . .
To whom their God has given grace!
To read, to fear, to hope, to pray—
To lift the latch and force the way;
And better had they ne'er been born
Who read to doubt or read to scorn.

—Sir Walter Scott

Contents

Contents

Poetic Spiritual Insight

Faith, Mighty Faith!

In God we live and move and breathe,
So trust in Him we must,
As He fulfills our purpose here . . .
Before we turn to dust!

For in him we live, and move, and have our being; as certain also of your own poets have said, For we are also his offspring. (Acts 17:28)

While we look not at the things which are seen, but at the things which are not seen: for the things which are seen are temporal; but the things which are not seen are eternal. (2 Cor. 4:18)

Now faith is the substance of things hoped for, the evidence of things not seen. (Heb. 11:1)

Webster's New World Dictionary describes faith as:
1. Unquestioning belief
2. Unquestioning belief in God

A Prayer of Moses the man of God. Lord, thou hast been our dwelling place in all generations. (Ps. 90:1)

A Song of degrees. I will lift up mine eyes unto the hills, from whence cometh my help. (Ps. 121:1)

Hast thou not known? hast thou not heard, that the everlasting God, the Lord, the Creator of the ends of the earth, fainteth not, neither is weary? there is no searching of his understanding. (Isa. 40:28)

Blessings

To our children—1978

Some folks count their blessings
In houses, cars, or land.
Others cherish clothing,
Or fame and fortune, grand!
Had we such temporal treasures,
Our hearts would still be cold;
For we find nothing precious
In houses, lands, or gold.

But we have been blessed with children . . .
A wealth of worth untold!
Each day they grow more precious
Though we are growing old.

Earth's treasures soon will vanish—
Our life is a short while;
We have known no greater treasure
Than a baby's morning smile!

Every good and perfect gift
Cometh from above,
Where the God who sends us children
Also sends us love.

Our very first arrival
Was a bouncing baby boy,
Followed by two sisters . . .
Three children to enjoy!

'Ere just a few more years had passed,
God sent another son.
With all the others older now—
This was the sweetest one.
How could God ever bless us more
Than sending child number four?
Just the perfect family . . .
Two boys for you, two girls for me!

Then we knew not the total score
Or how the Lord would bless us more.
Room to spare? Well no, not much . . .
Just room for highchairs, toys, and such.
Four children, active and alive—
All waiting now for number five!

'Twas secret yet for no one knew
that God would send not one but two!
Those darling little baby brothers
Were much enjoyed by all the others.

When life is finished, most folds find
Their earthly treasures left behind.
Not so with us; we'll say goodbye . . .
Then greet them all again on high!

First Thessalonians five, verse ten
Says we will dwell together again!
No wrath to face at the end of time
Through trusting Christ,
Taught in verse nine.

True wisdom has revealed somehow
That having blessings here and now
Can never, ever quite compare
To having them both *here* and *there*!

Lo, children are an heritage of the Lord: and the fruit of the womb is his reward. (Ps. 127:3)

Even a child is known by his doings, whether his work be pure, and whether it be right. (Prov. 20:11)

One generation shall praise thy works to another, and shall declare thy mighty acts. (Ps. 145:4)

O Lord our Lord, how excellent is thy name in all the earth! who hast set thy glory above the heavens. Out of the mouth of babes and sucklings hast thou ordained strength . . . (Ps. 8:1–2a)

See that ye refuse not him [God] that speaketh. For if they [the children of Israel] escaped not who refused him [Moses] that spake on earth, much more shall not we escape, if we turn away from him that speaketh from heaven. (Heb. 12:25)

And these words, which I command thee this day, shall be in thine heart: And thou shalt teach them diligently unto thy children, and shalt talk of them when thou sittest in thine house, and when thou walkest by the way, and when thou liest down, and when thou risest up. (Deut. 6:6–7)

But the mercy of the Lord is from everlasting to everlasting upon them that fear him, and his righteousness unto children's children; to such as keep his covenant, and to those that remember his commandments to do them. (Ps. 103:17–18)

And all thy children shall be taught of the Lord; and great shall be the peace of thy children. (Isa. 54:13)

I have no greater joy than to hear that my children walk in truth. (3 John 1:4)

For he established a testimony in Jacob, and appointed a law in Israel, which he commanded our fathers, that they should make them known to their children: That the generation to come might know them, even the children which should be born; who should arise and declare them to their children: That they might set their hope in God, and not forget the works of God, but keep his commandments. (Ps. 78:5–7)

For the promise is unto you, and to your children, and to all that are afar off, even as many as the Lord our God shall call. (Acts 2:39)

The Pilgrim Journey

Although at times we tremble,
through faith we understand,
The journey we are taking by God has been all planned.
There is one aim and purpose for all who service give;
Namely, that men in darkness may see the light and live!

As earth's night grows still darker,
God's children look toward home,
And though the storm clouds gather,
the heavenly groom will come!
With trumpet loud, He'll call us to be His holy bride,
And we in garments glorious will stand there by His side!

But if the Father tarry in sending back the Son,
He'll safely lead us homeward,
through death's door, one by one.
It really doesn't matter, for we have naught to fear,
Since He who is our Shepherd has promised to be near.

Within our precious Bible, God's love is plainly told,
And those who read, believing,
will find sweet gems of gold!
Though doubts sometimes possess us
when the way looks dark ahead,
We will still trust our Shepherd
who has risen from the dead!

His eye will always guide us; His hand will gently lead;
And those who sweetly trust Him
in pleasant pastures feed.
Though we should scale the mountains,

or walk softly through the vale,
The Holy Spirit leads us, and He can never fail.

Eye hath not seen nor ear heard, the things that yet await
For each of God's dear children within that pearly gate!
The troubles here that vex us will all have passed away—
And never more we'll sorrow in God's eternal day!
The Cross is sometimes heavy;
the nights are oft times long;
But one day, very soon now, we'll shout the victor's song.
Amid sweet rapture glorious, we will look upon the face
Of Him whose love has freely prepared for us a place,
Where we shall dwell together through all eternity;
For it is His desire that we with Him should be!

We'll worship in His presence,
sweet faith all changed to sight,
And never more remember the tears of earth's dark night.
How glad we'll be we served Him and tasted of His grace,
And never will regret it once we have seen His face!
Such grace does quite amaze us,
that the holy God would give
His only "Well Beloved" so sinful men might live!

Father, I will that they also, whom thou hast given me,
be with me where I am; that they may behold my glory,
which thou hast given me: for thou lovedst me before
the foundation of the world. (John 17:24)

Dearly beloved, I beseech you as strangers and pilgrims,
abstain from fleshly lusts, which war against the soul.
(1 Pet. 2:11)

The Robin's Song

When I was a child of tender years
And often filled with childish fears—
I'd suddenly hear the robin's song,
And the world seemed right
With nothing wrong!

My tears would vanish
And my heart be light
While my childish fears
All took to flight!
Peace came to me for my ears had heard
The joyful praise of a little bird!

Though my life has often been rearranged,
The robin's song has never changed.
It still has power to banish care,
Spreading happiness everywhere!

It takes me back to the days of old
And memories sweeter than pure gold.
To the days when I sat in our oak tree swing
And listened to the robin sing.

He sang to God sweet notes of praise.
Oh, those were blessed, carefree days!
After storm and showers
In the bright sun's rays
He still sings on, his song of praise.[1]

Sing unto the Lord, bless his name; show forth his salvation from day to day. (Ps. 96:2)

My beloved spake, and said unto me, Rise up, my love, my fair one, and come away. For, lo, the winter is past, the rain is over and gone; the flowers appear on the earth; the time of the singing of birds is come, and the voice of the turtle is heard in our land. (Song of Sol. 2:10–12)

Behold the fowls of the air: for they sow not, neither do they reap, nor gather into barns; yet your heavenly Father feedeth them. Are ye not much better than they? (Matt. 6:26)

Sing unto the Lord; for he hath done excellent things: this is known in all the earth. (Isa. 12:5)

Let every thing that hath breath praise the Lord. Praise ye the Lord. (Ps. 150:6)

Oh that men would praise the Lord for his goodness, and for his wonderful works to the children of men! (Ps. 107:8)

As a bird that wandereth from her nest, so is a man that wandereth from his place. (Prov. 27:8)

God created man to glorify Him and for fellowship with Him! Are we doing this?

Family Ties

Though ideas may be different
And at times we disagree,
Yet there remains a oneness
With those on our family tree!

In our hearts we have assurance
That nothing in this world supplies
The peace and joy and comfort
We possess through family ties!

Sometimes we laugh together;
Sometimes we join our tears;
In trials pray together,
And our Father calms our fears.

Today I checked the mailbox;
Found a note from precious kin—
"Don't forget to come and see us.
We are lonesome. Where have you been?"

So I polished up my dress shoes,
Pulled my suitcase from the shelf.
I'll soon be with the family . . .
Sure beats staying by myself!

My goodness, this bus travels slow!
Seems I've been on for hours.
At last I'm there. See, that's their house—
The one with all the flowers!

All hug and kiss and talk at once;
There is so much to say.

Must get a lot of things discussed
Before I go away.

The time has flown and I must leave;
Just hate those sad goodbyes;
Yet time and space can never break
Our precious family ties!

Believers are the *children* of *God!*

But when the fullness of the time was come, God sent forth his Son, made of a woman, made under the law, to redeem them that were under the law, that we might receive the adoption of sons. And because ye are sons, God hath sent forth the Spirit of his Son into your hearts, crying, Abba, Father. Wherefore thou art no more a servant, but a son; and if a son, then an heir of God through Christ. (Gal. 4:4–7)

I am as a wonder unto many; but thou art my strong refuge. Let my mouth be filled with thy praise and with thy honour all the day. Cast me not off in the time of old age; forsake me not when my strength faileth. (Ps. 71:7–9)

As cold waters to a thirsty soul, so is good news from a far country. (Prov. 25:25)

Better is a dinner of herbs where love is, than a stalled ox and hatred therewith. (Prov. 15:17)

These things have I spoken unto you, that my joy might remain in you, and that your joy might be full. This is my commandment, that ye love one another, as I have loved you. (John 15:11–12)

Standing for the Faith

Yes, some are standing for the faith;
They are sure that is God's will.
Standing firm upon the rock—
Motionless and still. Never bend their
Knees to pray, never bow their head.
There they stand upon the rock,
Motionless, as dead!

We must reveal the unknown God
To men who need Him so!
Never will they see our Christ
'Till we decide to go.

If we would stand firm for the faith
As our Holy Bible teaches,
We must spread the gospel news
As far as this earth reaches!

"Why call Me friend," our Savior said,
"And do not as I say?"
There is no time to tarry, friend.
The fields are ripe today!

He who becomes a friend of Christ
And follows His commands,
Though dark the way or fierce the foe,
This person truly stands.

Let us pray and give and go
As true soldiers obey His will,
Forever standing for the faith . . .
But never standing still!

The apostle Paul admonished believers: "That ye would walk worthy of God, who hath called you unto his kingdom and glory." (1 Thess. 2:12)

He hath showed thee, O man, what is good; and what doth the Lord require of thee, but to do justly, and to love mercy, and to walk humbly with thy God? (Mic. 6:8)

Wherefore take unto you the whole armour of God, that ye may be able to withstand in the evil day, and having done all, to stand. (Eph. 6:13)

But exhort one another daily, while it is called To day; lest any of you be hardened through the deceitfulness of sin. For we are made partakers of Christ, if we hold the beginning of our confidence steadfast unto the end. (Heb. 3:13–14)

Afterward he appeared unto the eleven as they sat at meat, and upbraided them with their unbelief and hardness of heart, because they believed not them which had seen him after he was risen. And he said unto them, *Go ye into all the world, and preach the gospel to every creature.* (Mark 16:14–15 emphasis added)

So then faith cometh by hearing, and hearing by the word of God. (Rom. 10:17)

And he [Abraham] believed in the Lord; and he counted it to him for righteousness. For when God made promise to Abraham, because he could swear by no greater, he sware by himself, saying, Surely blessing I will bless thee, and multiplying I will multiply thee. And so, after he had patiently endured, he obtained the promise. (Heb. 6:13–15)

I Am Thankful

Oh yes, I am so thankful
To my Father up above
Who has extended me His mercy
And has shown me His love!

For He sent the blessed Savior
To wash away my sin
And through Scripture, never changing,
Invites my faith in Him.

And not only for the future am I promised
Blessings rare, but day by day
God has promised, we have His tender care!

Dear Father, I am thankful;
My heart will sing Thy praise
For all Thy boundless blessings
Throughout eternal days!

O Praise the Lord, all ye nations: praise him, all ye people. For his merciful kindness is great toward us: and the truth of the Lord endureth for ever. Praise ye the Lord. (Ps. 117:1–2)

Consider the ravens: for they neither sow nor reap; which neither have storehouse nor barn; and God feedeth them: how much more are ye better than the fowls? (Luke 12:24)

Let all those that seek thee rejoice and be glad in thee: let such as love thy salvation say continually, The Lord be magnified. (Ps. 40:16)

Golden Anniversary Thoughts

God made them both, male and female,
And ordained they should be one . . .
A picture of God's church,
The bride of His dear Son!

God sensed the loneliness of man
And blessed him with a wife
To share the joys that He would send
And comfort him in strife!

Two hearts united become one
In holy bonds of love;
Though that was fifty years ago,
Blessings still come from above.

Can it be that fifty years so
Quickly sped away?
And that happy day your vows were said
Still seems like yesterday?

Do you wonder how that precious time
So quickly passed you by?
But it doesn't really matter
Since you are heading for the sky!

This world is not my home.
Yes, that's a precious thought,
And in God's presence you will see
Still more wonders wrought!

We cannot resist the conviction that this world is for us only the porch of another and more magnificent temple of the Creator's majesty.

—F. W. Faber (1814–1863), *Faith of Our Fathers*

But as it is written, Eye hath not seen, nor ear heard, neither have entered into the heart of man, the things which God hath prepared for them that love him. (1 Cor. 2:9)

But the path of the just is as the shining light, that shineth more and more unto the perfect day. (Prov. 4:18)

Marriage is honourable in all, and the bed undefiled: but whoremongers and adulterers God will judge. (Heb. 13:4)

O God, thou hast taught me from my youth: and hitherto have I declared thy wondrous works. (Ps. 71:17)

Now also when I am old and greyheaded, O God, forsake me not; until I have showed thy strength unto this generation, and thy power to every one that is to come. Thy righteousness also, O God, is very high, who hast done great things: O God, who is like unto thee! (Ps. 71:18–19)

Does It Really Matter?

Did that person mean to hurt me
With those words he quickly spoke?
Or was it meant to cheer me
And only as a joke?
Does it really matter
Since time speeds quickly past?
Life here will end, and I'll not care
When safely home at last!

It makes old Satan happy when God's
People get upset;
And he whispers to his demons,
"Look, there's one more we can get!"

So I'll think of one who loved me so
And begged for my forgiveness
While agonizing on the cross
Until His form was lifeless.

I have not "resisted unto blood"
Or loved in such a measure,
But I know to Him each soul is dear,
A rare and precious treasure!

Let me react to other's acts
As Christ has for my sin, with real and
True compassion, that they may enter in.
Yes, enter into peace and rest
Before their hope is gone
And opportunity has passed
To claim Christ as their own.

Will it really matter
When life has passed us by?
Why is it we're concerned with things?
Again, I ask you, why?

Should God decide to deal with us
In ways not understood,
We can be sure some day we'll know
He used it for our good!

Let us set our sights on things above
And never on the world,
And let the banner of Christ's love
To others be unfurled!
It has been said, "Earth has no pain
That heaven cannot heal."
The tests of life are always given
To make God's love more real.

The child of God will never find
True peace on this old earth
Until he sees that to the Lord
His soul alone has worth!

So does it really matter
If we forsake earth's treasure . . .
Since Christ has died,
And God has given forgiveness
Without measure?
It doesn't really matter,
For life speeds quickly past,
And soon we will not be here . . .
But safely home at last!

What Makes a Home?

A house might be a cottage or a mansion fair!
But the real important question is,
Does the Lord dwell there?
A house, 'tis said, becomes a home
When Jesus is a guest,
And harmony of family
Makes "home sweet home" the best!

Elegance and grandeur could be just an empty shell
Where hatred, tears, and angry words
Toward one another dwell.
And then again, a simple house can be a heavenly place—
And Jesus has a place.

So friend, it isn't hard to see
What makes a house a home;
It really isn't chandeliers,
Or beds of softest foam . . .
Picture windows, painted walls,
Or carpets in each room.
It's just caring for each other
That really makes a home!

So laugh and love and share
And enrich your dwelling place,
Rejoicing that God has prepared for you
An eternal home through grace!

I go to prepare a place for you. And if I go and prepare a
place for you, I will come again, and receive you unto
myself; that where I am, there ye may be also. (John
14:2b–3)

Life by Inches

"Life is hard by the yard;
By the inch, it's a cinch!"

Though this crazy little adage
Was phrased so long ago,
Through all my years of living,
I have always found it so.

The troubles of tomorrow
And the tears of yesterday
I must never, ever carry
As I walk along life's way!

For God who gives us life
Gives us moments one by one.
As we live each tiny second,
Soon we find our day is done!

If taken by the inches,
Life really isn't hard—
So why, oh why, do I insist
On living by the yard?

Why do I borrow troubles
From the days that are ahead
When I could enjoy the present
And praise the Lord instead?

Perhaps someday I'll be convinced
That life is not really hard;
When I live it by the inches
Instead of by the yard![2]

Trust in the Lord, and do good; so shalt thou dwell in the land, and verily thou shalt be fed. (Ps. 37:3)

But now, O Lord, thou art our father; we are the clay, and thou our potter; and we all are the work of thy hand. (Isa. 64:8)

Take therefore no thought for the morrow: for the morrow shall take thought for the things of itself. Sufficient unto the day is the evil thereof. (Matt. 6:34)

I have been young, and now am old; yet have I not seen the righteous forsaken, nor his seed begging bread. (Ps. 37:25)

The Lord knoweth the days of the upright: and their inheritance shall be for ever. (Ps. 37:18)

Daisies

Have you ever seen the daisies
Nod their heads beneath the sun?
And have you ever pondered
The perfection of each one?

As the summer breezes gently pass,
They smile and nod and sway
To brighten hearts of travelers
Who chance to pass their way!

They seem to say, "Hello there!
So glad you're passing by."
And, "We would like to come along,
If we were not so shy."

Have you ever seen the daisies
And wondered at the power
That formed those tiny petals
Of perfection on each flower?

Though man has traveled swiftly
To the moon and then returned,
The secrets of the daisies
He never yet has learned.

Lovely flowers can be fashioned
By man's hand . . . of silk and lace,
But none tug at our heartstrings
Like a living daisy face!

Consider the lilies how they grow: they toil not, they spin not; and yet I say unto you, that Solomon in all his glory was not arrayed like one of these. (Luke 12:27)

Let the field be joyful, and all that is therein: then shall all the trees of the wood rejoice (Ps. 96:12)

Before the Lord: for he cometh, for he cometh to judge the earth: he shall judge the world with righteousness, and the people with his truth [word]. (Ps. 96:13)

God is a righteous judge!

Heading Home

Oh, praise the Lord, we are heading home—
Never, ever more to roam.
Sing, oh saints, with heart and soul
While pressing toward your final goal!

Raise the victory banner high;
Soon we take off for the sky!
No machine man could invent
Would withstand our fast ascent!

In the twinkling of an eye,
Immortal bodies upward fly!
Cares of earth will dissipate
Before we reach the pearly gate.

Oh, praise the Lord, we are heading home,
Never, ever more to roam.
Loved ones we've lost will greet us there,
But not a one so dear or fair
As our blessed, blessed Lord
Who has given us His word . . .
"Because I live, ye too shall live."
These words He spoke, and they are true.
Let us not fear but walk in faith—
We are heading home when life is through!

The valley may be long and deep;
The mountains may be tall and steep;
But, praise the Lord, we are heading home,
Never, ever more to roam!

For God hath not appointed us to wrath, but to obtain salvation by our Lord Jesus Christ, Who died for us, that, whether we wake or sleep, we should live together with him. (1 Thess. 5:9–10)

All that the Father giveth me shall come to me; and him that cometh to me I will in no wise cast out. For I came down from heaven, not to do mine own will, but the will of him that sent me. And this is the Father's will which hath sent me, that of all which he hath given me I should lose nothing, but should raise it up again at the last day. And this is the will of him that sent me, that every one which seeth the Son, and *believeth* on him, may have everlasting life: and I will raise him up at the last day. (John 6:37–40 emphasis added)

Babies

Babies are precious
And babies are sweet;
From their soft fuzzy heads
To the toes of their feet!
At times they will coo
And at times stay awake,
Sending forth cries
That make your head ache!

But when he smiles in the morning,
You will thrill to his face
And swear that no other
Could e'er take his place.

Years have a way of passing too fast,
And in no time at all,
Childhood has passed!
Dandelions clutched in a chubby fist
During bygone days
Will be sadly missed.

So cherish each day with your baby so small,
And thank God for this gift,
For He sends them all!

Every good gift and every perfect gift is from above, and
cometh down from the Father of lights, with whom is
no variableness, neither shadow of turning. (James 1:17)

Lo, children are an heritage of the Lord: and the fruit of
the womb is his reward. (Ps. 127:3)

As thou knowest not what is the way of the spirit, nor how the bones do grow in the womb of her that is with child: even so thou knowest not the works of God who maketh all. (Eccl. 11:5)

A Tribute to Dad

Dear Daddy, I am only four . . .
My feet are still so very small,
But I love to slip on your big boots
And dream that I have grown tall!

That I am a daddy just like you,
Helping my little boy tie his shoe.
Fixing a toy or playing ball
Or hanging a picture on Mother's wall.

I dream of the day I will be like you
Because there is nothing that you can't do.
Though I dream of the day when I'll be tall,
Right now I am happy being small
For there is nothing I would rather do
Than live and walk with a dad like you!

So I'll eat my meat and spinach too,
And grow and grow to be tall like you.
Then my boots will fit in the steps you've trod,
And your Bible and prayers help me walk with God!

But there is not a thing I would rather do
Than someday be a dad like you.

When I was a child, I spake as a child, I understood as a child, I thought as a child: but when I became a man, I put away childish things. (1 Cor. 13:11)

And, ye fathers, provoke not your children to wrath: but bring them up in the nurture and admonition of the Lord. (Eph. 6:4)

A Tribute to Son

We have walked together many days
And blessed each other numerous ways.
I only hope I taught you well
As I brushed away each tear that fell!

Your favorite little books I read
And kissed you as you ran to bed.
Then I read a little from God's Word
And prayed that you would trust the Lord!

My son, I am growing older now
With the etch of years upon my brow,
But I still praise God for sending you
To bless and love my whole life through!

You have taught me many things, dear boy,
Of patience, wisdom, peace, and joy!
To help correct each childish sin,
I used the rod of discipline.

Though this was always hard to do,
The Lord taught me, as I taught you!
Together, son, as we tread earth's sod,
Let us put our hands in the hand of God,
As I thank the Lord on bended knee
That He gave a son like you to me.

If ye endure chastening, God dealeth with you as with sons; for what son is he whom the father chasteneth not? But if ye be without chastisement, whereof all are

partakers, then are ye bastards, and not sons. Further-
more we have had fathers of our flesh which corrected
us, and we gave them reverence: shall we not much rather
be in subjection unto the Father of spirits, and live? For
they verily for a few days chastened us after their own
pleasure; but he for our profit, that we might be partak-
ers of his holiness. (Heb. 12:7–10)

Correction is grievous unto him that forsaketh the way:
and he that hateth reproof shall die. (Prov. 15:10)

For whom the Lord loveth he correcteth; even as a fa-
ther the son in whom he delighteth. (Prov. 3:12)

My son, keep thy father's commandment, and forsake
not the law of thy mother: . . . For the commandment is
a lamp; and the law is light; and reproofs of instruction
are the way of life. (Prov. 6:20, 23)

Children, obey your parents in all things: for this is well
pleasing unto the Lord. (Col. 3:20)

Withhold not correction from the child: for if thou
beatest him with the rod, he shall not die. Thou shalt
beat him with the rod, and shalt deliver his soul from
hell. (Prov. 23:13–14)

My son, forget not my law; but let thine heart keep my
commandments: For length of days, and long life, and
peace, shall they add to thee. (Prov. 3:1–2)

Sunshine

Singing and laughter, heartaches and tears,
In each of our lives these constitute years.
God's love interwoven is shaping our lives,
Revealing His beauty as our selfish will dies.
Though we prefer sunshine, our Father sends strife
And His sweet Holy Spirit to work in our life.

Then we cry, "Dear Father, does this show Your love
When we prayed for sunshine sent down from above?"
"Ah, precious child, My will you must learn.
Were it not for the valleys, to Me you'd not turn.

"You may never reach heaven
If you walk all alone;
I must guide your footsteps . . .
You'll see, when you've grown."

Take Christ for your guide as you journey alone.
He'll comfort in sorrow, and you will become strong!
He'll snatch you from pitfalls of sin and of woe,
Send courage for trials, and you'll sing as you go.
He will pray for you too when dark shadows you meet.
Just trust Him and rest at His crucified feet.
When earth's hour has ended and eternity begun,
You'll have sunshine forever
With God's blessed Son.

Then shall the righteous shine forth as the sun in the
kingdom of their Father. Who hath ears to hear, let him
hear. (Matt. 13:43)

Verily, verily, I say unto you, he that heareth my word, and *believeth* on him that sent me, hath everlasting life, and shall not come into condemnation; but is passed from death unto *life*. (John 5:24 emphasis added)

Praise Him

Oh, that men would praise the Lord
For His goodness and His power;
For His loving care and guidance
Every moment, every hour!

Though men's hearts be yet far from Him,
And in darkness, many stray,
God never fails to bless them
With the rain or sun each day.

He is Lord of all the harvest,
And by Him all things consist;
His mercy never faileth . . .
Though His grace men still resist.

He who hung the earth on nothing,
Put the planets in their sphere,
Never slumbers, never sleepeth;
But sees all things far and near.

Praise Him, praise Him, all ye people!
Quickly turn your back on sin.
Lay aside your heavy burden
And invite the Savior in.

He will never force an entrance
But is pleading ever more.
As He knocks and knocks again,
Will you open your heart's door?
If Christ has come to seek admission
And you have asked Him to abide,

Then praise will swell within you,
Bringing victory over pride!

Real content will be your portion
As you walk the higher plain,
And your heart will then be thankful
For good health or even pain;
For we know our all-wise Father
Allows not one thing in vain.

If all men would praise the Lord
For His majesty and love,
They would anticipate Christ's coming
And long to dwell above!

While I live will I praise the Lord: I will sing praises unto my God while I have any being. (Ps. 146:2)

Oh that men would praise the Lord for his goodness, and for his wonderful works to the children of men! (Ps. 107:8)

My voice shalt thou hear in the morning, O Lord; in the morning will I direct my prayer unto thee, and will look up. (Ps. 5:3)

I was glad when they said unto me, Let us go into the house of the Lord. (Ps. 122:1)

The Lord hath done great things for us; whereof we are glad. (Ps. 126:3)

I will bless the Lord at all times: his praise shall continually be in my mouth. (Ps. 34:1)

A Family Book

The family is a unit,
First ordained by God's decree,
Who will honor their Creator,
If they dwell in unity.

Father has the headship,
Loving Mom with all his might;
Together, seeking godly wisdom,
They will guide the children right.

The mind of man would never learn
Without literature to read;
And if a book could teach man knowledge,
Faith and hope must be its creed!

Every family must remember
That the Holy Scriptures say,
Man must not live by bread alone
But take God's Word each day!

The Bible is a family book,
Chock-full of sound advice,
And all who read it have a hope
Though Satan may entice.

Parents ought to be obeyed,
The Book of Proverbs teaches.
A son, when grown, should always bless
Where e'er his influence reaches!

A daughter too can love the Lord,
Be obedient to her mother;

Wash the dishes, make the bed,
Or rock her baby brother.

Even a child, the Bible says,
Is known by his deeds.
His mind is changing every day,
And he learns through what he reads!

Many families today
Are filled with consternation.
Because men have not obeyed God's Word,
We have become a sinful nation!

Fearful children everywhere
Know not where to look,
Because when they were growing up,
None have read the family book!

O Lord, I know that the way of man is not in himself: it is not in man that walketh to direct his steps. (Jer. 10:23)

Husbands, love your wives, even as Christ also loved the church, and gave himself for it. (Eph. 5:25)

When our Savior was tempted by Satan on the Mount, He quoted from Deuteronomy 8:3: "But he answered and said, It is written, Man shall not live by bread alone, but by *every word* that proceedeth out of the mouth of God" (Matt. 4:4).

Every way of a man is right in his own eyes: but the Lord pondereth the hearts. (Prov. 21:2)

Children, obey your parents in the Lord: for this is right. (Eph. 6:1)

What Is a Son?

A son, at birth, is a precious life
From heaven's portals sent
With waving arms and an angel smile,
All sweet and innocent.

At two he becomes an engineer,
Building towers from his blocks.
Between three and four
He will shut the door
And manage his shoes and socks!

At six he's a soldier tall and straight,
Marching off to school
Through our swinging gate!

By the age of eight he's a diplomat,
Curled up with a book
And the family cat.
In two more years he's a fisherman
With a freckled nose and a face of tan!

At twelve he's a pilot
As he flies his kite,
Still adding inches to his height.

The years have flown, and I had scarcely seen
Until today he is a teen!
Tomorrow he will be a man—
And to mold his life, I no longer can.
So help me, Lord, to lead and guide
My precious son while he is by my side!

And all thy children shall be taught of the Lord; and great shall be the peace of thy children. (Isa. 54:13)

Train up a child in the way he should go: and when he is old, he will not depart from it. (Prov. 22:6)

Wherewithal shall a young man cleanse his way? by taking heed thereto according to thy word. (Ps. 119:9)

A wise son maketh a glad father: but a foolish son is the heaviness of his mother. (Prov. 10:1)

A wise son heareth his father's instruction: but a scorner heareth not rebuke. (Prov. 13:1)

Hear [listen], O my son, and receive my sayings; and the years of thy life shall be many. (Prov. 4:10)

He that refuseth instruction despiseth his own soul: but he that heareth reproof getteth understanding. (Prov. 15:32)

Fathers, provoke not your children to anger, lest they be discouraged. (Col. 3:21)

But when the fullness of the time was come, *God sent forth his Son,* made of a woman, made under the law, to redeem them that were under the law, that we might receive the adoption of sons. (Gal. 4:4–5 emphasis added)

That all men should honour the Son, even as they honour the Father. He that honoureth not the Son honoureth not the Father which hath sent him. (John 5:23)

Mothers

To keep the home tidy and do things for others,
The Lord in His wisdom has provided mothers!
She will hop up at night when baby is new.
She will rock him, if ill, all the night through.

Mothers are people who should receive medals
With hearts that are pure as white daisy petals.
Their kisses can heal our pains and our aches
And comfort our hearts when we've made mistakes.

Though we call her mother, she is really a queen
Who stirs up sweet goodies like you've never seen!
She washes our clothes, hangs them in the breeze,
Then with needle and thread patches my trouser knees.

She vacuums the carpets and scrubs up the floors,
Helps us with our coats when we play out of doors!
Sometimes she might even become referee,
For children are not always good, you'll agree.

Amid many problems, Mom's words of praise
Inspire our dad to face future rough days!
When springtime arrives, Mother puts in some seeds;
Then Daddy takes over to keep out the weeds.

Most mothers love beauty, especially ours,
So the breeze in our yard wafts the fragrance of flowers!

When at day's end I kneel by my bed,
Mother is there to hear prayers being said.
Sisters are precious, as also are brothers,
But praise be to God for giving us mothers!

He maketh the barren woman to keep house, and to be a joyful mother of children. Praise ye the Lord. (Ps. 113:9)

As one whom his mother comforteth, so will I comfort you; and ye shall be comforted in Jerusalem. (Isa. 66:13)

Who can find a virtuous woman? for her price is far above rubies. The heart of her husband doth safely trust in her, so that he shall have no need of spoil. She will do him good and not evil all the days of her life. (Prov. 31:10–12)

No man is poor who has a godly mother!
—Abraham Lincoln

Circus Day

Smile awhile; put off that frown.
Today is circus day in town!
The big tent is up and made quite secure.
Should wind or rain come,
It will safely endure.
Sounds of a circus ring out through the air!
Soon children and adults will congregate there,
Watching acrobats fly on their high trapeze,
Hanging by their teeth or knees!
It never fails to bring a thrill
And gives our sleeping spines a chill!

See the lion trainer in the ring?
He's there to do a daring thing! Puts his head in
The lion's jaws and calmly shakes
Hands with his paws.

A lady fair rides the elephant,
Using one leg only. What a stunt!
Look, there is a polar bear in the ring—
Along comes her baby, the cutest thing.

Wow! Looky here, another attraction—
Cowboys and horses ready for action.
The band gives a blast as they enter the ring.
Aren't those prancing stallions a beautiful thing?

You'll not find a circus without a gay clown
Doing all sorts of tricks; he's up and he's down!
He talks and acts stupid while he skips and he skids,
And, of course, always tries to sell balloons to kids.

A seal may look dumb, but great poise he shows.
See him balance that ball on the tip of his nose!
Peanuts and popcorn, candy bars too
Later on will become a temptation to you.

Your money's not gone yet, but that time will come
And leave you deciding it's time to head home.
Your day at the circus would have been a real blast,
If only your change hadn't vanished so fast.

I said in mine heart, Go to now, I will prove thee with
mirth, therefore enjoy pleasure: and, behold, this also is
vanity. (Eccl. 2:1)

Joy and Praise

Joy is not found in earthly things
For these soon fade away.
The things that thrilled us yesterday
May bring no joy today.

But children of the heavenly King,
Redeemed through grace alone,
Through faith possess an inner joy
That the world has never known.

True joy is more than happiness
And more than present thrills.
It is a gentle whisper,
Which the Lord Himself instills!

A still, small voice within the heart,
God's peace and comfort bring.
And those who know their Savior lives
Just cannot help but sing!

With Christ alive within us
We have reason to be glad!
And our hearts go out to others,
Folks disheartened and so sad.

So praise Him, all ye children.
Yes, be joyful every day!
Bow your heads in adoration;
Sing His praise and humbly pray.

Thou wilt show me the path of life: in thy presence is fullness of joy; at thy right hand there are pleasures for evermore. (Ps. 16:11)

I have made the earth, and created man upon it: I, even my hands, have stretched out the heavens, and all their host have I commanded. (Isa. 45:12)

Autumn

Is there another season
That is quite as nice as fall?
No! I am convinced beyond a doubt . . .
This is the best of all!

I view a farmer's tall corn field
With ripe ears hanging low
And am assured of God's great power;
'Twas He that made it grow!

The acorns in the meadow
Have turned from green to brown;
And I hear the rustling oak leaves
That are gently falling down.

White fleecy clouds surround a flock
Of southbound honking geese;
While navigating as a group,
Their cries reveal their peace!

The morning sun reflects upon
The leaves of gold and red;
Among their vines, all turned to brown,
Orange pumpkins raise their head!

Young, hopeful farmers
With calves and pigs
Are heading for the fair,
And with great anticipation
Plan to win some ribbons there!

Happy youngsters, with school bags new,
Wave goodbye to house and swing,
Expecting new adventures,
Which "back-to-school" should bring.

Do you think there ever was
Another season quite as grand
As autumn with its bounties
God has provided on our land?

Yet we so often gather in
The good harvest God has given;
But we forget all thanks are due
Our Father up in heaven!

While the earth remaineth, seedtime and harvest, and cold and heat, and summer and winter, and day and night shall not cease. (Gen. 8:22)

He hath made every thing beautiful in his time . . . (Eccl. 3:11a)

Honour the Lord with thy substance, and with the firstfruits of all thine increase: So shall thy barns be filled with plenty, and thy presses shall burst out with new wine. (Prov. 3:9–10)

Giving thanks always for all things unto God and the Father in the name of our Lord Jesus Christ. (Eph. 5:20)

Tiny Oaks

Midst growing shrubs and living wood,
In the mystic forest a great oak stood.
'Till one windy day, 'neath a gusty blast,
The great oak shivered and her acorns cast!

One little acorn was heard to fret,
As it hit the sod, all cold and wet,
"Mr. Gusty Wind, why did you come by
And leave me lying here to die?
It was so pleasant on the tree;
Now the cold, damp sod will cover me.
I cannot see the starry sky
Or face the sun as it passes by."

But the great oak said, "Little seed, take heart,
For trees and God can never part.
The rain will fall and the sun will shine,
Then your roots will sprout;
Only give God time."
Though his heart was sad, and he wore a frown,
That little acorn settled down.
Some large oak leaves who saw him there,
Shivering, all cold and bare,
Gently covered him, we're told;
And he fell asleep in the bitter cold.

Now the sun is warm, and the snow has gone;
Little acorn needs no covers on!
The forest dresses all its own
With mossy greens and flowers strewn!

Busy gray squirrel chatters now
And sprightly leaps from bough to bough.
While mother robin starts her nest,
Then can't decide which limb is best.
Little acorn has a tender root
And through the leaves sends a bright green shoot!
Stretching his neck for a better view,
He takes a look at life anew
And with all his might shouts, "I'm a tree!
Mother Oak, please look at me!"
But a mossy stump beside him stood
As he took his place in the mammoth wood.
Then Tiny waved, in glad surprise,
For there were more oaks just his size!
No doubt they had slept all winter too,
For what else can an acorn do?
They waved and hummed and began to play!
Oh, what a grand and glorious day.

All soon began the "grow big" race
And schemed to take their parent's place.
The violets laughed with the trillium
As they joined the little oaks in fun.

Jack-in-the-pulpits squealed with glee
And peeked from under their hats to see
This fun-filled forest rendezvous
Then quickly joined the party too.

Then tiny oak felt strong and free
And very proud to be a tree!
Many years have passed;
Now the wild deer flees
From the hunter's darts to the great oak trees.

When "Gusty Wind" blows an arctic blast,
She is sheltered there and safe at last.
She will quench her thirst at the
Bubbling spring and feed on almost anything.
Mr. Hare sneaks out, as bunnies do,
Hears the night owl crying, "Who, who, who?"

Now tiny oak is a strong, huge tree;
To his lofty limbs the eagles flee.
But tiny oak will never know
It was the mighty God who made him grow.

And he that sat upon the throne said, Behold, I make all things new. And he said unto me, Write: for these words are true and faithful. And he said unto me, It is done. I am Alpha and Omega, the beginning and the end. I will give unto him that is athirst of the fountain of the water of life freely. He that overcometh shall inherit all things; and I will be his God, and he shall be my son. (Rev. 21:5–7)

For every beast of the forest is mine, and the cattle upon a thousand hills. I know all the fowls of the mountains: and the wild beasts of the field are mine. (Ps. 50:10–11)

Sing, O ye heavens; for the Lord hath done it: shout, ye lower parts of the earth: break forth into singing, ye mountains, O forest, and every tree therein: for the Lord hath redeemed Jacob, and glorified himself in Israel. (Isa. 44:23)

My Friend

I had a friend in yesteryear
Who very rarely shed a tear.
She laughed and sang, as hand in hand
We ran and skipped o'er the meadow grand!

I thrilled at the sight of the daisies there
And plucked one for Ann's golden hair.
She smiled her thanks, as my hand she took,
Saying, "Mother will say, 'How nice you look!'"

After we'd stopped at the spring to drink,
We skipped to the song of the bob-o-link!
I spied and picked some wild berries.
Ann laughingly said, "They taste like cherries."

When night came on at the close of day,
Ann knelt by her bed and was heard to pray,
"Thank You, Lord, for this lovely day and
Bless my friend, with whom I play!
And, when our lifetime here is through,
May we live together again with You."

Her God and her Savior long since called her home,
And I know she is beckoning me to come.
Precious memories of Ann still fill my mind,
But I scarcely recall . . . my friend was blind!

A man that hath friends must show himself friendly: and
there is a friend that sticketh closer than a brother. (Prov.
18:24)

The glory of friendship is not the outstretched hand, or the kindly smile, or the joy of companionship; it is the spiritual inspiration that comes to one when he discovers that someone believes in him and is willing to trust him with his friendship.

—Ralph Waldo Emerson

High and Low

Calla lilies, Easter lilies, and lilies of the valley
All humbly bow to dandelions,
which spring up in the alley.
The honeybee while buzzing by
Stops at our rose bush sweet,
But she'll never pass the bright moss roses,
Creeping near the street!
See those tall and stately yellow faces
That watch the sun . . . all in their places.
As twilight falls their heads hang low
To greet the marigolds below!

Forget-me-nots can not grow tall;
The Lord is pleased to see them small.
Their petals form a sea of blue,
Which reflects God's love to me and you.
A straw flower is the strangest thing,
Yet in winter time much joy 'twill bring.
I took some to a friend when ill,
A little void in his heart to fill!

The morning-glories above my door
Will never, ever thrill me more
Than the tulips and crocus of early spring;
They fairly cause my soul to sing!
Geraniums are placed on memorial plots
Of loved ones we must bury;
Yet seldom will you discover there
The Bells of Mistress Mary.

Petunias will grow, it has been said,
Even in an onion bed!

There they will weather the autumn frost
To beautify fall at any cost.
A flower pinned on one's lapel,
Especially a carnation, will place a man—
though rich or poor—
In a state of elevation!

Though flowers have no lips and ears,
Or eyes with which to see,
Yet in a way I can't explain,
They speak a lot to me!
Even as flowers, so God made man
To fill his place in a mighty plan!
Regardless if we are great or small,
He has a purpose for us all.
Though we may think our place is low,
God put us here so we can grow.
So let us trust His grace and power,
For He designed each lovely flower!

A man that hath friends must show himself friendly: and
there is a friend that sticketh closer than a brother. (Prov.
18:24)

He Knows His Own

You will need Him in a troublesome day,
So seek His face and humbly pray.
When testings come, not understood,
Just take them quickly to the Lord!

Though you in darkness walk one day,
Christ will be guiding all the way.
When testings come, not understood,
The Scriptures still say, "God is good!"

He knows the path you take each day
And walks beside you along the way.
When you choose to let Him guide,
You'll find Him walking by your side.

But if you try to shut Him out,
There is nothing left but fear and doubt.
So will you walk in doubt and fear,
Or trust the Lord, who walks so near?

He knoweth them that trust in Him,
And those who choose to walk in sin.
He wants to be your shepherd, friend,
So let Him guide you until the end.

Many, O Lord my God, are thy wonderful works which
thou hast done, and thy thoughts which are to us-ward:
they cannot be reckoned up in order unto thee: if I would
declare and speak of them, they are more than can be
numbered. (Ps. 40:5)

For the eyes of the Lord are over the righteous, and his ears are open unto their prayers: but the face of the Lord is against them that do evil. (1 Pet. 3:12)

For the eyes of the Lord run to and fro throughout the whole earth, to show himself strong in the behalf of them whose heart is perfect toward him. (2 Chron. 16:9a)

But he knoweth the way that I take: when he hath tried me, I shall come forth as gold. (Job 23:10)

Hereby know we that we dwell in him, and he in us, because he hath given us of his Spirit. (1 John 4:13)

The Lord is good, a strong hold in the day of trouble; and he knoweth them that trust in him. (Nah. 1:7)

God not only knows us after we are born but *before* we are born!

My substance was not hid from thee, when I was made in secret, and curiously wrought in the lowest parts of the earth. Thine eyes did see my substance, yet being unperfect; and in thy book all my members were written, which in continuance were fashioned, when as yet there was none of them. (Ps. 139:15–16)

Let God be God!

Of the Lord

Remember, God's child, if you possibly can—
All testings are of the Lord and not man!
And they are never to penalize
But to turn our faces toward the skies!

As gifts of love from our Father's hand,
They strengthen our faith and help us stand.
Remember, dear child, God makes no mistakes
And always returns more than He takes!

When He calls us to suffer, for a reason unknown,
We may rest assured that our spirits have grown.
To our enemy we will never succumb
As we travel along the road toward home!

Every piece of armor must be put to use;
If in this men fail, they are without excuse.
Remember, God's child, if you possibly can—
All testings are of the Lord and not man.

We are in a battle, but it is the Lord's,
Who defines our armor in the simplest words.
Faith is our shield, and the Scriptures our sword;
Salvation, our helmet, is a gift from the Lord.
Righteousness, as our breastplate,
Will shield us from darts
That Satan will hurl, full force,
Toward our hearts!

Prayer is our powerline directed to God,
Who lovingly carries our heaviest load.

For we do not wrestle against flesh and blood
But the powers of evil in a dark, sinful world.

But God supplies grace and multiplied peace,
Plus love and protection that never will cease.
Victory is ours through faith in His Son,
Whose death on the cross paid sin's debt for each one.
So remember, God's child, if you possibly can—
Life's testings are of the Lord and not man.

The Lord can handle it; just trust Him!

And he said, Hearken ye, all Judah, and ye inhabitants
of Jerusalem, and thou king Jehoshaphat, Thus saith the
Lord unto you, Be not afraid nor dismayed by reason of
this great multitude; for the battle is not yours, but God's.
(2 Chron. 20:15)

We serve the same God!

For we wrestle not against flesh and blood, but against
principalities, against powers, against the rulers of the
darkness of this world, against spiritual wickedness in
high places. (Eph. 6:12)

Love

Love is a very mysterious thing
That can cause a weeping heart to sing!
It is not a thing we can see or feel,
But in a strange, true way, we know it's real.

When the tiny babe feels his mother's arms,
He is comforted quickly of all alarms.
A bouquet of roses on Mother's Day
Proves Father's love more than words can say!

Dandelions clutched in a chubby fist
During by-gone days are sadly missed.
Valentine greetings say it too
As all our cards and letters do.

Birthday cakes with candles lit
Have a wonderful way of showing it.
A gift all tied with a bow so fair
Is definite proof that love's been there.

A strong young man with steady feet,
Guiding the aged across the street,
Lets others know that love is here;
One word of comfort can dry a tear!

A gingerbread cookie shared with her dolly
Is proof it lives in the heart of Molly!
Two brothers are happy and things are all right,
For a mutual hug followed their fight!

A man and a maiden with golden hair
Holding hands in the moonlight
Reveals love is there.

Christ's love excels that of father or mother,
And He's always closer than sister or brother.
If you've never met this friend from above,
You are missing the power of greatness of love!
God gave His Son on the cross to die;
Overwhelming truth: love is not a lie!

The ultimate love was shown to us in Jesus Christ:

Whom having not seen, ye love; in whom, though now you see him not, yet *believing,* ye rejoice with joy unspeakable and full of glory. (1 Pet. 1:8 emphasis added)

We love Him because He first loved us!

By this shall all men know that ye are my disciples, if ye have love one to another. (John 13:35)

He that loveth not knoweth not God; for God is love. In this was manifested the love of God toward us, because that God sent his only begotten Son into the world, that we might live through him. (1 John 4:8–9)

Behold, what manner of love the Father hath bestowed upon us, that we should be called the sons of God: therefore the world knoweth us not, because it knew him not. (1 John 3:1)

For the Son of man is come to seek and to save that which was lost. (Luke 19:10)

Finished

"It is finished," Jesus cried
As He gave up the ghost.
Every farthing He had paid,
Demanded of the lost.
His visage was so marred,
None recognized His face!
It was my sin that put Him there;
He suffered in my place!

One malefactor railed on Him,
Saying, "Save thyself and us!"
But one decided to believe;
Christ saved his soul through trust!
While blood flowed from His wounded side,
His beard, the wicked plucked.
Hateful men spit in His face,
His robe they gained through luck.

"Father, forgive them," our Savior prayed,
"They know not what they do.
Other sheep have I, not of this fold;
I die to save them too!"

God's Word fulfilled, none broke His bones;
They saw that He had died.
'Twas Satan taught their souls to hate;
Their hearts he filled with pride.

But God, the Father, planned it all,
That men He could redeem,
Bring back to fellowship with Him;
Thus banish Satan's scheme!

"It is finished," Jesus cried.
God gave His Son through grace.
Our love and service we will give,
Then one day see His face!

And almost all things are by the law purged with blood; and without shedding of blood is no remission. (Heb. 9:22)

The blood of Christ covers (takes care of) every sin ever committed!

For God so loved the world, that he gave his only begotten Son, that whosoever believeth in him should not perish, but have everlasting life. (John 3:16)

And again, I will put my trust in him. And again, Behold I and the children which God hath given me. Forasmuch then as the children are partakers of flesh and blood, he also himself likewise took part of the same; that through death he might destroy him that had the power of death, that is, the devil; and deliver them who through fear of death were all their lifetime subject to bondage. (Heb. 2:13–15)

And one of the malefactors which were hanged railed on him, saying, If thou be Christ, save thyself and us. But the other answering rebuked him, saying, Dost not thou fear God, seeing thou art in the same condemnation? And we indeed justly; for we receive the due reward of our deeds: but this man hath done nothing amiss. (Luke 23:39–41)

Come now, and let us reason together, saith the Lord: though your sins be as scarlet, they shall be as white as snow; though they be red like crimson, they shall be as wool. (Isa. 1:18)

It Took a Lamb

Since the days of righteous Abel,
Who was slain by wicked Cain,
Men have been bringing sacrifice,
But all have come in vain.

It took a Lamb, God's spotless Lamb;
No other gift would do.
But when He died, God was satisfied—
And the veil was rent in two!

The door to heaven opened wide
To all who will confess
Their fruitless works not good enough
To meet God's righteousness!

No righteous deeds that we may do
Could cause our souls to live;
But when we take our sins to Christ,
God always will forgive.

It took a Lamb, God's spotless Lamb,
No other gift would do.
But when He died, God was satisfied—
And the veil was rent in two!

Oh, praise His name!
And laud His fame!
God's spotless, holy Lamb.
Through faith in His atoning blood,
God's precious child I am.

He was oppressed, and he was afflicted, yet he opened not his mouth: he is brought as a lamb to the slaughter, and as a sheep before her shearers is dumb, so he openeth not his mouth. (Isa. 53:7)

Behold the Lamb of God, which taketh away the sin of the world. (John 1:29b)

Neither by the blood of goats and calves, but by his own blood he entered in once into the holy place, having obtained eternal redemption for us. (Heb. 9:12)

Forasmuch as ye know that ye were not redeemed with corruptible things, as silver and gold, from your vain conversation received by tradition from your fathers; but with the precious blood of Christ, as of a lamb without blemish and without spot. (1 Pet. 1:18–19)

Today man needs a spiritual rebirth to enter God's presence. "Jesus answered and said unto him, Verily, verily, I say unto thee, *Except a man be born again, he cannot see the kingdom of God*" (John 3:3 emphasis added).

Faith in God's Lamb (Jesus Christ) produces that spiritual rebirth! "But as many as received him, to them gave he power to become the sons of God, even to them that *believe* on his name: Which were born, not of blood, nor of the will of the flesh, nor of the will of man, but of God" (John 1:12–13 emphasis added).

For the law made nothing perfect, but the bringing in of a better hope did; by the which we draw nigh unto God. (Heb. 7:19)

The Lord hath sworn, and will not repent, Thou art a priest *for ever* after the order of Melchizedek. (Ps. 110:4 emphasis added)

No Time Today

I heard a voice whisper to my heart,
"Oh, child, today is the time to start
Reading the Bible, God's Word from heaven,
To your dear little son,
Whom God has given!"

But I am too busy to read and pray;
I have so many things to do today!
Yet I heard again that gentle voice,
Saying, "It's up to you. You must
Make a choice. Will he run with the world
Or walk with the Lord, finding sweet peace
Through God's holy Word?"

Then my little one turned away in sorrow, asking,
"Mommy, will you read tomorrow?"
"Yes, I'll not be so busy tomorrow,"
I said, placing my hand on his curly head.
So, with anticipation, he raced away,
Waiting in faith for another day!

But I had no peace in my heart that night;
I quickly arose with the morning light
To kneel by my bed and there confess
My sin of too much "busy-ness."

I heard not a sound as I arose to my feet
And entered the room where our child lay asleep.
But there was no more time to read or pray,
For an angel had stolen his soul away!

Right there, in great sorrow,
I resolved to pray
And not keep Jesus waiting another day!

For the Father judgeth no man, but hath committed all judgment unto the Son. (John 5:22)

Whom send I to judge them? Whom but thee,
Viceregent Son; to thee I have transferred
All judgment, whether in Heaven, or Earth, or Hell.
— John Milton, *Paradise Lost,* Book X

Therefore to him that knoweth to do good, and doeth it not, to him it is sin. (James 4:17)

As for man, his days are as grass: as a flower of the field, so he flourisheth. For the wind passeth over it, and it is gone; and the place thereof shall know it no more. (Ps. 103:15–16)

What man is he that liveth, and shall not see death? shall he deliver his soul from the hand of the grave? Selah. (Ps. 89:48)

The days of our years are threescore years and ten; and if by reason of strength they be fourscore years, yet is their strength labour and sorrow; for it is soon cut off, and we fly away. (Ps. 90:10)

For we are strangers before thee, and sojourners, as were all our fathers: our days on the earth are as a shadow, and there is none abiding. (1 Chron. 29:15)

Would You See the Glory?

I am the Lord; that is my name: and my glory will I not give to another. (Isa. 42:8a)

A burning bush, yet unconsumed,
Revealed God's glorious power
To Moses who removed his shoes
In that sacred, solemn hour!

Would you see the glory, friend,
The glory of the Lord?
And know the blessed Savior,
He who is the living Word?

"Behold, a virgin shall conceive,
And a holy child be born."
Isaiah spoke; it came to pass—
We call it Christmas morn!
Come with me to a wedding feast
In Cana of Galilee, and taste
The water turned to wine;
'Twas the best could ever be!

Can you stop just for a moment, friend?
To hear Him bless the bread
And a boy's few tiny fishes,
Which five thousand hungry fed?

See Martha standing by a grave
And Mary, weeping, too. See Lazarus,
Bound in grave clothes,

As Christ gives him life anew!
See Jesus approach a ship at sea
As His disciples, frightened, cry!
Hear Him speak in gentle tone,
"Be not afraid; it is I!"

Have you met the centurion's servant,
Whose palsy Jesus cured
Through the mighty power of God,
As only once, He spoke the word?
There was a man, blind from birth;
Christ gave him sight, 'tis true!
How deep would be your gratitude,
If the man had been you?

A woman touched His garment
And rejoiced within her soul
As He said to her, "My daughter,
Thy faith hath made thee whole."

Remember Mary Magdalene, who came
To weep and pray? When lo! She saw
The mighty stone at the tomb was rolled away!
Oh, you *will* see the glory, friend;
The glory of the Lord, when you read
The Scripture's pages
And *believe* their every word!

Let thy work appear unto thy servants, and thy *glory*
unto their children. (Ps. 90:16 emphasis added)

That, according as it is written, He that glorieth, let him
glory in the Lord. (1 Cor. 1:31)

Our Savior Lives!

Though flowers fade
And their petals fall,
As time slips swiftly by;
We have a hope that never dims . . .
Our Savior lives on high!
"Because I live, ye too shall live."
His words will come to pass.
We'll leave behind this fleshly robe,
Put on His righteousness.

Safe in Him

As you sail o'er life's sea,
Take Christ as your guide.
Remember He promised
To stay close to your side.
When storm clouds appear
And the waves toss you high,
You've no need to fear;
The Lord hears your cry!
Storms always pass
And new days begin,
So rest in this truth—
You are kept safe in Him!

Let that therefore abide in you, which ye have heard from the beginning. If that which ye have heard from the beginning shall remain in you, ye also shall continue in the Son, and in the Father. And this is the promise that he hath promised us, even eternal life. (1 John 2:24–25)

Behold, I show you a mystery; We shall not all sleep, but we shall all be changed. (1 Cor. 15:51)

In a moment, in the twinkling of an eye, at the last trump: for the trumpet shall sound, and the dead shall be raised incorruptible, and we shall be changed. For this corruptible must put on incorruption, and this mortal must put on immortality. So when this corruptible shall have put on incorruption, and this mortal shall have put on immortality, then shall be brought to pass the saying that is written, Death is swallowed up in victory. O death, where is thy sting? O grave, where is thy victory? (1 Cor. 15:51–55)

O Lord God of hosts, who is a strong Lord like unto thee? or to thy faithfulness round about thee? Thou rulest the raging of the sea: when the waves thereof arise, thou stillest them. (Ps. 89:8–9)

For thou hast been a strength to the poor, a strength to the needy in his distress, a refuge from the storm, a shadow from the heat . . . (Isa. 25:4a)

The righteous shall flourish like the palm tree: he shall grow like a cedar in Lebanon. Those that be planted in the house of the Lord shall flourish in the courts of our God. (Ps. 92:12–13)

And the work of righteousness shall be peace; and the effect of righteousness quietness and assurance for ever. (Isa. 32:17)

The name of the Lord is a strong tower: the righteous runneth into it, and is safe. (Prov. 18:10)

Celebrating

We celebrate a lot of things
While traveling through this life;
We celebrate when a fine young man
Receives a bride as wife!

Then if a little one arrives
We celebrate his birth;
And thank the Lord for every gift
Bestowed to us on earth.

Today it is time to celebrate
The greatest day of all!
Better far than Christmas
Or Thanksgiving in the fall.

Today the mighty power of God
Rolled away the stone
So man could look
But could not find
Christ's body in that tomb!

Thank You, God, for showing us
Such mercy and such love.
We know Christ died on earth for us
So we can live above!

Yes, that resurrection morning
Gave us victory from the grave.
Today Christ lives with God, His Father,
And has been given power to save!

What a day to celebrate!
It far exceeds the rest. Just think!
God loves us all so much,
He gave His very best.

But this man, because he continueth ever, hath an unchangeable priesthood. Wherefore he is able also to save them to the uttermost that come unto God by him, seeing he ever liveth to make intercession for them. (Heb. 7:24–25)

For the Father judgeth no man, but hath committed all judgment unto the Son. (John 5:22)

For as the Father raiseth up the dead, and quickeneth them; even so the Son quickeneth whom he will. (John 5:21)

An Easter Wish

Wishing you the joy and peace
That the truth of Easter brings!
When I recall that Jesus lives,
My glad heart always sings.

We have an advocate above
Who always intercedes
And the blessed Holy Spirit
Who reveals to Him our needs.

Not only that, God's precious Word
Says Christ will come again,
And we can know without a doubt,
We *will* be with Him then!

And when they had fulfilled all that was written of him, they took him down from the tree, and laid him in a sepulchre. But God raised him from the dead: And he was seen many days of them which came up with him from Galilee to Jerusalem, who are his witnesses unto the people. (Acts 13:29–31)

He is not here: for he is risen, as he said. Come, see the place where the Lord lay. (Matt. 28:6)

So then after the Lord had spoken unto them, he was received up into heaven, and sat on the right hand of God. (Mark 16:19)

And [Jesus was] declared to be the Son of God with power, according to the spirit of holiness, by the resurrection from the dead. (Rom. 1:4)

Obedience

The meaning of obedience is
Seeking not our will but only His.
His, who gave His Son through grace,
That men might have a hiding place!

Believers who God's Word obey
Will not lead other souls astray.
Their light will shine;
Their works abound, ever marching on
To higher ground!
But if on lower plain we walk,
Few folks will listen to our talk.
They need to see a life that's real,
Before they at the cross will kneel.

Great miracles we need not do;
Just walk with God, who will bring
Us through. Stand firm through trials,
Large and small, seeking God's purpose
In it all.
Our heavenly Father makes no mistakes.
His love is there, though our heart breaks.
If we but trust, His Word obey,
He will soon reveal a better way.

Obedience results in joy,
But lack of it can soon destroy
The alien's faith in our God of grace,
His holy wrath one day to face!

Though worldly scenes attract today,
Their gold and glitter soon fade away.

The pleasures of sin last but a season.
This alone is a good reason
That we, who believe, also obey,
Not living only for today.
Our pilgrimage is on foreign sod,
Traveling home to the city of God!

Does a walk of obedience really pay?
And will it profit to kneel and pray?
Peace will be our reward and gain,
If we walk with God on the higher plain.
And peace is really all men need
To find true happiness indeed!

Whoso is wise, and will observe these things, even they shall understand the lovingkindness of the Lord. (Ps. 107:43)

For as by one man's disobedience many were made sinners, so by the obedience of one shall many be made righteous. (Rom. 5:19)

Though he were a Son, yet learned he obedience by the things which he suffered. (Heb. 5:8)

And Samuel said, Hath the Lord as great delight in burnt offerings and sacrifices, as in obeying the voice of the Lord? Behold, to obey is better than sacrifice, and to hearken than the fat of rams. (1 Sam. 15:22)

The sacrifices of God are a broken spirit: a broken and a contrite heart, O God, thou wilt not despise. (Ps. 51:17)

And why call ye me, Lord, Lord, and do not the things which I say? (Luke 6:46)

His Workmanship

In days gone by we all had walked
According to the world;
In sins and trespasses were dead,
No victory flag unfurled.

But now our spirits quickened of God,
No longer serve the flesh.
Children of wrath we are no more,
With new hearts, pure and fresh!

We know our God is rich in grace,
In mercy, love, and kindness,
For He has quickened us together,
Removed our doubt and blindness.

We have not done this of ourselves,
But God, through the Holy Ghost.
For could we work our way to heaven,
Some would have cause to boast.

We are the workmanship of God,
Created in Christ Jesus,
Ordained to walk in works of love
Before the world that sees us!

And in the ages yet to come,
God plans to show His kindness
Toward us, through Jesus Christ our Lord,
Whose death removed our blindness.

And you hath he quickened, who were dead in trespasses and sins: Wherein in time past ye walked according to the course of this world, according to the prince of the power of the air, the spirit that now worketh in the children of disobedience: Among whom also we all had our conversation in times past in the lusts of our flesh, fulfilling the desires of the flesh and of the mind; and were by nature the children of wrath, even as others. But God, who is rich in mercy, for his great love wherewith he loved us, even when we were dead in sins, hath quickened us together with Christ, (by grace ye are saved;) and hath raised us up together, and made us sit together in heavenly places in Christ Jesus: That in the ages to come he might show the exceeding riches of his grace in his kindness toward us through Christ Jesus. (Eph. 2:1–7)

Fellowship

The Lord is faithful, this we read
Within His Word, our sword.
To fellowship we have been called
Through Jesus Christ our Lord!

"Love one another," God hath said;
Be comforting and kind.
Let joy and peace reign in each heart
And God's grace fill each mind.

Lord, let us always steadfast be,
Praise God with hearts so glad.
Believe the apostles' doctrine,
Who all things common had.

Oh, my friend, have you not heard
That true love for each other
Will cover a multitude of sins
And strengthen a dear brother?

How else can we prove to the world
With its need that we all
Belong to God's family indeed?

Paul said: "I thank my God for you
As I in prayer do bow,
For we have had sweet fellowship
From the beginning until now."

Though great or least of all the saints,
To each, His grace God giveth,

To reveal the mystery of Christ,
Who made each thing that liveth.

By Jesus Christ, our living Lord,
God, all things hath created.
And soon He will come, the Son of God,
For whom so long we have waited.

(For the life was manifested, and we have seen it, and bear witness, and show unto you that eternal life, which was with the Father, and was manifested unto us;) That which we have seen and heard declare we unto you, that ye also may have fellowship with us: and truly our fellowship is with the Father, and with his Son Jesus Christ. (1 John 1:2–3)

God is faithful, by whom ye were called unto the fellowship of his Son Jesus Christ our Lord. (1 Cor. 1:9)

If there be therefore any consolation in Christ, if any comfort of love, if any fellowship of the Spirit, if any bowels and mercies, Fulfill ye my joy, that ye be likeminded, having the same love, being of one accord, of one mind. (Phil. 2:1–2)

And they continued steadfastly in the apostles' doctrine and fellowship, and in breaking of bread, and in prayers. . . . And all that believed were together, and had all things common. (Acts 2:42, 44)

And this is his commandment, That we should believe on the name of his Son Jesus Christ, and love one another, as he gave us commandment. (1 John 3:23)

My Contented Kitten

I have a fluffy, furry kitten,
Contented as can be.
She never gets down in the dumps
Or has the blues like me.
She never, ever holds a grudge
Or gets her feelings hurt.
Never says, "I'll pay her back,"
Or, "That cat did me dirt."
She cleans her soft paws everyday
And licks her velvet fur.
If you tiptoe quietly and close,
You will hear her gentle purr!

Her favorite ball is Grandma's yarn,
And quite a web she will weave.
But never once in all her life
Has she tried to deceive.
Come, see my fluffy, furry kitten,
Contented as can be.
Peaceful, gentle, happy too;
She teaches things to me!

He that is slow to anger is better than the mighty; and
he that ruleth his spirit than he that taketh a city. (Prov.
16:32)

Better it is to be of an humble spirit with the lowly, than
to divide the spoil with the proud. (Prov. 16:19)

But godliness with contentment is great gain. (1 Tim.
6:6)

Two Become One

Two hearts united become one,
According to God's plan.
From Adam's rib God made a wife—
Then gave her back to man.

God knew that it would not be good
For man to live alone.
Now he is free to choose a bride
And make her all his own!

In bonds of holy matrimony,
Two hearts in love unite;
Together seek God's grace and power
To spread the gospel light.

Though life is never free of care,
When tests and trials come,
Faith in their Savior and God's Word
Will build a Christian home!

Love and patience, peace and grace,
Each new day they must borrow,
Trusting the Lord, who is always near,
In every joy and sorrow.

Each marriage man performs on earth
Speaks of heaven above,
Where Christ's own bride,
His redeemed church,
Will dwell with Him in love!

Whosoever putteth away his wife, and marrieth another, committeth adultery: and whosoever marrieth her that is put away from her husband committeth adultery. (Luke 16:18)

Know ye not that the unrighteous shall not inherit the kingdom of God? Be not deceived: neither fornicators, nor idolaters, nor adulterers, nor effeminate, nor abusers of themselves with mankind. (1 Cor. 6:9)

Marriage is honourable in all, and the bed undefiled: but whoremongers and adulterers God will judge. (Heb. 13:4)

And the Lord God caused a deep sleep to fall upon Adam, and he slept: and he took one of his ribs, and closed up the flesh instead thereof; and the rib, which the Lord God had taken from man, made he a woman, and brought her unto the man. (Gen. 2:21–22)

Therefore shall a man leave his father and his mother, and shall cleave unto his wife: and they shall be one flesh. (Gen. 2:24)

Whoso findeth a wife findeth a good thing, and obtaineth favour of the Lord. (Prov. 18:22)

And the man that committeth adultery with another man's wife, even he that committeth adultery with his neighbour's wife, the adulterer and the adulteress shall surely be put to death. (Lev. 20:10)

Arizona

I think that man will never know
How God can make a cactus grow
In the desert sand so bare and dry,
'Neath the blazing sun in a clear blue sky!

They not only grow in the soil so bare
But send forth flowers with fragrance rare!
Amid tumbleweed and sage brush hills,
Man can see God's touch if his heart so wills.

From the saguaro flower to the prickly pear,
What lack of proportion in the blossoms they bear!
Was man ever blessed with such poise and grace?
Or the lightening speed of the road-runner's pace?

Hear the gentle call of a mourning dove
As you meditate on the Father's love.
Past the distant plain and the mountain's height,
By faith we see our God of light.

He made each living thing that grows,
And the thoughts of every soul He knows.
In Mark, chapter six, verse thirty-one
We read some words spoken by God's Son.

"Come aside with Me into a desert place
and rest awhile; receive strength and grace."
So let us take time to thank the Lord
As we meditate upon His Word.

And our faith in the Creator can never fail,
If we have walked in spring along the Apache Trail!
To view Grand Canyon is the hopeful fate
Of sightseeing tourists who enter the state.
This state of awesome beauty rare
Leaves indelible memories, once you have
Traveled there!

And he said unto them, *Come ye yourselves apart into a desert place, and rest a while*: for there were many coming and going, and they had no leisure so much as to eat. (Mark 6:31 emphasis added)

Hats on Parade

Most ladies wear hats
To accent their clothes;
Topped with some feathers
Or perhaps a rose.
Hats made of fur, fabric, or lace
In someone's wardrobe will soon
Take their place!

Yankee Doodle's riding hat
Had a feather in;
His obvious intention was
Some charming girl to win!

Folks employed in factories
Wear hard hats on their head
For safety purposes, we are told,
So they won't end up dead!

Tiny perky hats of white
Are usually worn by nurses;
Such little ones are never worn
To match their style of purses.

Some wear wide brims to shield the heat
While others keep out cold.
Black top hats graced the noble heads
Of aristocrats of old!

In a certain period of time,
When Ivy League was style,
To nab the guy who wore one,
Some gals would run a mile!

A Scotch plaid hat with narrow brim
Is suitable for golf;
While berry pickers like to keep
A wide brim on their shelf.

There is a little beanie cap;
This looks right on a monkey.
Few folks care to wear these;
Reminds us of a donkey!

I've seen a crazy, peaked hat
Designed to fit the dunce.
The student forced to wear one
Will do so only once!

A purpose for the cowboy's hat?
I haven't heard about it
Except his attire would not look right,
Were he to ride without it.

Four-cornered hats with tassels on
Appear at graduation,
After which our students seek
Their place in our great nation!

The fireman has a unique hat,
Which small boys rave about.
This hat must definitely be worn
When fires are put out!

The policeman's hat identifies
And also looks distinguished.
The circus clown, in a funny hat,
His identity relinquished.

There are army hats and navy too,
For men who sail the ocean blue.
Hats to be worn on Halloween
And Irish hats in shamrock green!

Hats of every form and kind,
As you dream on, will come to mind.
But never one with more renown
Than a ruling monarch's stately crown!

Thy kingdom is an everlasting kingdom, and thy dominion endureth throughout all generations. (Ps. 145:13)

I will extol thee, my God, O king; and I will bless thy name for ever and ever. (Ps. 145:1)

Who is this King of glory? The Lord of hosts, he is the King of glory. Selah. (Ps. 24:10)

Behold, a king shall reign in righteousness, and princes shall rule in judgment. (Isa. 32:1)

And the loftiness of man shall be bowed down, and the haughtiness of men shall be made low: and the Lord alone shall be exalted in that day. (Isa. 2:17)

The Lord hath prepared his throne in the heavens; and his kingdom ruleth over all. (Ps. 103:19)

The Lord is in his holy temple, the Lord's throne is in heaven: his eyes behold, his eyelids try, the children of men. (Ps. 11:4)

Because I will publish the name of the Lord: ascribe ye greatness unto our God. He is the Rock, his work is perfect: for all his ways are judgment: a God of truth and without iniquity, just and right is he. (Deut. 32:3–4)

Yet have I set my king upon my holy hill of Zion. I will declare the decree: the Lord hath said unto me, Thou art my Son; this day have I begotten thee. (Ps. 2:6–7)

The Common Cold

Our baby son was very ill when only four months old,
And when we had the problem checked,
Doc said: "The common cold!
You really need not be concerned."
But what a cold can do, we hadn't learned.
"Just take him home and keep him warm;
Pour liquids down his throat.
And if at any given time his crying can't be hushed,
Just give some liquid aspirin
Or else a small one, crushed."

That night our little darling slept,
His angel face all peace.
Just liquids and some aspirin
Had brought him sweet release!

Today he's like new and as good as gold.
We have killed the bug called the common cold!

Next day he slept long past morning light,
But when he awoke both eyes were tight.
I prepared a cloth under soft, warm steam.
When it touched his eyes, he began to scream!
No need for concern—hadn't we been told
Our youngster has the common cold?
After several days of tears and pain,
Our lovely child could see again!
As we gazed upon his baby face,
We knew no other could take his place.

The lights are out, our house all dark.
What's that I hear? Sounds like a bark!

You guessed correct; it was our baby's cry,
And we thought for sure he soon would die!

Doc called it croup. "No cause for alarm."
Guess the common cold can do no harm.

We are at the drugstore now, you see.
Our child needs humidity.
I have five dollars and his Dad has ten—
Just enough to get him well again!

We are glad that croup has gone away.
He is sleeping now from dusk 'til day!
We are not concerned for we've been told,
"No problem, just a common cold."

Pray tell, are those his screams I hear?
And why is he pulling on his ear?
Now we understand what an ear can do.
Kept the family up the whole night through.
But we won't worry none or fret.
It's the common cold,
And he'll lick it yet!

His temp is up to one-o-three,
And his body as limp as it can be.
At the hospital the nurses tell
That our little boy will soon be well!
His antibiotics are so strong;
Pneumonia just can't stay long.

And sure enough, every word was true;
We left with joy, as most folk do!

Our bill was four hundred dollars today.
We are glad it wasn't a longer stay.
But we will long remember when we were told,
Not to be alarmed at the common cold!

And he [Jesus] arose out of the synagogue, and entered into Simon's house. And Simon's wife's mother was taken with a great fever; and they besought him for her. And he stood over her, and rebuked the fever; and it left her: and immediately she arose and ministered unto them. Now when the sun was setting, all they that had any sick with divers diseases brought them unto him; and he laid his hands on every one of them, and healed them. (Luke 4:38–40)

When the even was come, they brought unto him many that were possessed with devils: and he cast out the spirits with his word, and healed all that were sick. (Matt. 8:16)

Precious Child

Precious child, I know . . .
I see every tear;
I feel every heartache;
I know every fear.
I, when so burdened,
In Gethsemane prayed;
Then trusted My Father,
Walked on unafraid.

Accepting His will,
I walked on to the cross,
Counting earth's treasures
As nothing but dross.

Only pray and believe;
Precious child, I know
That testings and trials
Cause small faith to grow!

Though fleshly desires
Would tie you to earth,
With love I will guide
Since your spiritual birth!

Precious child, I pray every hour for you;
And I know every trial that
You have come through.
It was for you I took every dart.
Child, can't you see
Why you're close to My heart?

So let My sweet Spirit speak
To your soul.
You'll arrive safely home,
For I am in control.

I pray for them: I pray not for the world, but for them
which thou hast given me; for they are thine. . . . Sanc-
tify them through thy truth: thy word is truth. (John
17:9, 17)

Be careful for nothing; but in every thing by prayer and
supplication with thanksgiving let your requests be made
known unto God. (Phil. 4:6)

Born to Die

At this holy season,
Let us give God the glory
While glad bells chime out
The old Christmas story!

As we celebrate His nativity,
Let us not forget dark Calvary.
That tiny Babe was born to die;
There is no other reason why
He laid His head in manger stall
But to redeem us one and all!

This greatest of gifts was lovingly given
Through the goodness and mercy
Of our Father in heaven.
Shepherds rejoiced on the first Christmas Day,
As that holy Babe in a stable lay!
Kings gave Him gifts and honored His name;
To rejoice at His birth, many miles they came!

Will we today give Him honor and glory
As glad bells chime out
The old Christmas story?
Let our gifts to each other be a symbol of love,
As that first Christmas gift
God sent from above!

Oh, may we today give Him honor and glory
While the glad bells peel forth
The old Christmas story.

For unto us a child is born, unto us a son is given: and the government shall be upon his shoulder: and his name shall be called Wonderful, Counselor, The mighty God, The everlasting Father, The Prince of Peace. (Isa. 9:6)

For the wages of sin is death; but the gift of God is eternal life through Jesus Christ our Lord. (Rom. 6:23)

God gave us eternal life when He gave His Son to pay all our debt of sin—when He shed His blood on Calvary's cross.

That humble birth in the manger of Bethlehem was not Christ's beginning. Listen to His own words:

I have glorified thee on the earth: I have finished the work which thou gavest me to do. And now, O Father, glorify thou me with thine own self with the glory which I had with thee before the world was. (John 17:4–5)

Calvary

For a price far less than a
Shekel of gold, Judas, the traitor,
Himself hath sold! For filthy lucre
His soul he'd sell, then spend
Eternity in hell!

And many a man on earth today
Is selling his soul for an idol gay.
Be it wealth or pleasure or next of kin,
If preferred to Christ,
In God's sight, 'tis sin.

When our Savior trod
Up Calvary's road with His back bent low
'Neath the cross's load—
Though His heart was heavy
With the sins of man,
In obedience He carried out
The Father's plan.

That Lamb of God in meekness stood
While cruel hands placed Him
On that cross of wood.
He endured the cross,
Despised the shame because
He for this purpose came!

God loved His Son and hid His face;
What boundless love,
What matchless grace!
That He who formed the world and man
Should thus devise salvation's plan.

He paid our debt in full not part.
Lord, teach us to love Thee
For what Thou art—
The blessed way, the truth, the life;
The ransom paid to end all strife.
What boundless love!
What matchless grace!
Salvation free for Adam's race!

Facing death by crucifixion, Jesus prayed, "Now is my soul troubled; and what shall I say? Father, save me from this hour: but for this cause came I unto this hour" (John 12:27).

But he was wounded for our transgressions, he was bruised for our iniquities: the chastisement of our peace was upon him; and with his stripes we are healed. (Isa. 53:5)

All we like sheep have gone astray; we have turned every one to his own way; and the Lord hath laid on him the iniquity of us all. (Isa. 53:6)

God's Thoughts on Riches

Charge them that are rich in this world, that they be not highminded, nor trust in uncertain riches, but in the living God, who giveth us richly all things to enjoy. (1 Tim. 6:17)

Men turn their back on God and faith
When they covet earthly loot.
For the *love* of money, God hath said,
Gives evil a strong root.

God's faithful servant is not promised
A dwelling huge and great.
In constant struggle for worldly gain,
He will sell his soul to fate.

If our attitude toward others
Who have more wealth than us
Contains a mite of envy,
Then we are covetous.

A man's life consisteth not
In the things that he possesses;
But godliness with contentment
Will reveal what he professes.

Though a righteous man have very little,
Psalm Thirty-Seven states,
This is far better in God's eyes
Than the wealth of reprobates!

In chapter eleven and verse four
In the Book of Proverbs we read,
Riches profit not in the day of wrath,
But righteousness delivereth indeed.

One man may heap great treasures up,
Yet still be poor in heart.
While another, having but daily bread,
In God's riches shares a part!

There was a ruler, very rich,
Who asked Christ what to do,
To be assured that heaven's gate
Would open to him too. Christ said
That he should sell his goods
And give unto the poor;
But he turned away with saddened
Heart and followed Christ no more.

If you think you would be happy,
If your riches God would double—
Remember, Proverbs teaches
Great riches could spell trouble!

The Bible states that wisdom
Is more precious than pure gold;
And understanding should be chosen
Over silver, we are told.

He that handleth a matter wisely
Shall receive good from the hand of God,
And he shall be happy daily,
As he treads this foreign sod!

So let us not labor to be rich
Or consider ourselves wise;
For earthly treasures soon grow wings
And take off for the skies!

A faithful man of God
With blessings shall abound;
But in men who hasten to be rich,
Innocence will not be found.

So labor not to gather up treasures
Upon earth, where wicked thieves
Could steal them
Or rust corrupt their worth.

There was a man God called a fool,
Who had no room to store
All the treasure he had saved—
So he built barns to hold yet more!

To choose a good name instead of riches
And God's favor over gold
Will bring the heart contentment;
This in Proverbs, we are told.

The Holy Scriptures teach indeed
That the Lord will provide our every need!
Let us not love the world
Or the things that are in it,
But glorify God and praise Him each minute!

For the love of money is the root of all evil: which while
some coveted after, they have erred from the faith, and

pierced themselves through with many sorrows. (1 Tim. 6:10)

As the partridge sitteth on eggs, and hatcheth them not; so he that getteth riches, and not by right, shall leave them in the midst of his days, and at his end shall be a fool. (Jer. 17:11)

Thou shalt not covet thy neighbour's house, thou shalt not covet thy neighbour's wife, nor his manservant, nor his maidservant, nor his ox, nor his ass, nor any thing that is thy neighbour's. (Exod. 20:17)

A little that a righteous man hath is better than the riches of many wicked. (Ps. 37:16)

Riches profit not in the day of wrath: but righteousness delivereth from death. (Prov. 11:4)

There is that maketh himself rich, yet hath nothing: there is that maketh himself poor, yet hath great riches. (Prov. 13:7)

Is the Lord Jesus Christ the treasure of your heart, or do you love the things of this world?

And when he heard this, he was very sorrowful: for he was very rich. And when Jesus saw that he was very sorrowful, he said, *How hardly shall they that have riches enter into the kingdom of God!* (Luke 18:23–24)

Better is little with the fear of the Lord than great treasure and trouble therewith. (Prov. 15:16)

How much better is it to get wisdom than gold! and to get understanding rather to be chosen than silver! (Prov. 16:16)

He that handleth a matter wisely shall find good: and whoso trusteth in the Lord, happy is he. (Prov. 16:20)

Labour not to be rich: cease from thine own wisdom. Wilt thou set thine eyes upon that which is not? for riches certainly make themselves wings; they fly away as an eagle toward heaven. (Prov. 23:4–5)

A faithful man shall abound with blessings: but he that maketh haste to be rich shall not be innocent. (Prov. 28:20)

And I will say to my soul, Soul, thou hast much goods laid up for many years; take thine ease, eat, drink, and be merry. But God said unto him, Thou fool, this night thy soul shall be required of thee: then whose shall those things be, which thou hast provided? (Luke 12:19–20)

Lay not up for yourselves treasures upon earth, where moth and rust doth corrupt, and where thieves break through and steal: But lay up for yourselves treasures in heaven, where neither moth nor rust doth corrupt, and where thieves do not break through nor steal: For where your treasure is, there will your heart be also. (Matt. 6:19–21)

A good name is rather to be chosen than great riches, and loving favour rather than silver and gold. The rich and poor meet together: the Lord is the maker of them all. (Prov. 22:1–2)

Love not the world, neither the things that are in the world. If any man love the world, the love of the Father is not in him. (1 John 2:15)

Accidents

After it has happened,
We are sure to ask: "What for?
How could I be so stupid
And bump into that door?"

Why do we answer telephones
And not turn off the burners?
Oh, will we ever graduate
Or always be just learners?

I felt helpless and embarrassed
And made a stupid show
When I descended the last step
With still one left to go!

The dog upset my ladder;
Of course, my paint can spilled.
But I am still very thankful;
So glad I wasn't killed!

Forgot to open up the door
When backing from the garage . . .
My husband thought, *Is this for real?
Or is it a mirage?*

Perhaps I'll see some signs around
And learn to read them yet.
Just sat down to rest a bit—
On a painted bench, still wet!

Accidents just happen 'cause
We don't stop to think.

Strangest thing 'bout accidents—
They happen in a wink!

There really are no accidents with God. He uses all things to bless us in His own time and way.

And we know that all things work together for good to them that love God, to them who are the called according to his purpose. (Rom. 8:28)

And not only so, but we glory in tribulations also: knowing that tribulation worketh patience. (Rom. 5:3)

And patience, experience; and experience, hope. (Rom. 5:4)

Words

Though "talk is cheap," we often say,
Our words affect someone, some way.
They honor God or help the devil.
They comfort one or send forth evil.
Our tongue, God says, is like a fire,
Used often to our own desire!
Before we speak, let us take heed;
What could result in word or deed?
Will we help one laugh or make one weep?
Or much offend one of God's dear sheep?

Help us, dear Lord, to stop and pray
Before a harmful word we say.
Let not a single word be spoken
To cause a friend's heart to be broken.
Words past our lips we can not retrieve,
Though hard we pray and long we grieve.

"By thy words thou shalt be justified
Or by them be condemned."
This was spoken by the Lord,
So take good heed, my friend!
Advice on speaking can be found
In chapter three of James.
Such words of wisdom far excel
Our human thoughts and aims!
Speak gently as life's road you trod
And lead another on toward God.
A words is such a little thing,
But it can cause a soul to sing!
So speak in love and a kindly way,

For God records the words we say.
When life's path for someone is too rough,
Our comforting words may be enough
To help that one see the face of God,
Turn from deep despair to upward trod.
What power is held in a little word:
Will you speak for Satan or for the Lord?

For he that will love life, and see good days, let him refrain his tongue from evil, and his lips that they speak no guile. (1 Pet. 3:10)

The wicked is snared by the transgression of his lips: but the just shall come out of trouble. (Prov. 12:13)

The tongue of the just is as choice silver. (Prov. 10:20a)

Be not rash with thy mouth, and let not thine heart be hasty to utter any thing before God: for God is in heaven, and thou upon earth: therefore let thy words be few. (Eccl. 5:2)

A soft answer turneth away wrath: but grievous words stir up anger. (Prov. 15:1)

Whoso keepeth his mouth and his tongue keepeth his soul from troubles. (Prov. 21:23)

I said, I will take heed to my ways, that I sin not with my tongue. (Ps. 39:1a)

A fool's mouth is his destruction, and his lips are the snare of his soul. (Prov. 18:7)

Let the *words* of my mouth, and the meditation of my heart, be acceptable in thy sight, O Lord, my strength, and my redeemer. (Ps. 19:14 emphasis added)

Poem of Life

Man is born to trouble
As the sparks do upward fly.
But the blessing of the Lord
Maketh men rich by and by!

Every child born of God
Shall life eternal know,
And through partaking of God's Word,
That spiritual babe shall grow!

Every child who heareth well
The message of God's love
Will now receive eternal life
And continue it above!

If you believe God's Word, my friend,
You may know without a doubt
That Christ will welcome you above;
Not one will be shut out!

All that the Father giveth me shall come to me; and him
that cometh to me I will in no wise cast out. (John 6:37)

It is the spirit that quickeneth; the flesh profiteth noth-
ing: the words that I speak unto you, they are spirit, and
they are life. (John 6:63)

These things have I written unto you that believe on the
name of the Son of God; that ye may know that ye have
eternal life, and that ye may believe on the name of the
Son of God. (1 John 5:13)

Seeing his [man's] days are determined, the number of his months are with thee, thou hast appointed his bounds that he cannot pass. (Job 14:5)

Yet man is born unto trouble, as the sparks fly upward. (Job 5:7)

The blessing of the Lord, it maketh rich. (Prov. 10:22a)

Being born again, not of corruptible seed, but of incorruptible, by the word of God, which liveth and abideth for ever. (1 Pet. 1:23)

As newborn babes, desire the sincere milk of the word, that ye may grow thereby. (1 Pet. 2:2)

For God so loved the world, that he gave his only begotten Son, that whosoever *believeth* in him should not perish, but have everlasting life. (John 3:16)

Verily, verily, I say unto you, He that heareth my word, and believeth on him that sent me, hath everlasting life, and shall not come into condemnation; but is passed from death unto life. (John 5:24)

That which we have seen and heard declare we unto you, that ye also may have fellowship with us: and truly our fellowship is with the Father, and with his Son Jesus Christ. (1 John 1:3)

The Death of a Believer

I would not ask that you should mourn,
Knowing now my soul has flown.
Is not my life now hid with God?
Have I not trusted in His Word?

The Word that lit my path below,
Now with my soul, I see and know.
The Book is true; God sent His Son
That all to Him in faith may come.

And oh, this bliss, with Him to be
Throughout all eternity!
I tell you now, my life and soul,
Which I did yield to God below . . .
He will bring again within my form
On that great resurrection morn!

So sorrow not that I have gone
Because my soul to God has flown;
But ask thyself if thou art whole.
Have you trusted Christ to save
Your soul?
He's pleading yet as time goes by:
"Oh, come to Me; why will ye die?"

He shed His blood to cleanse your sin.
Oh, soul, will you not let Him in?
Already He has prepared your place,
But you must first accept His grace.
Trust not thyself but trust His love,
And thou shalt live with Him above!

Behold, what manner of love the Father hath bestowed upon us, that we should be called the sons of God: therefore the world knoweth us not, because it knew him not. Beloved, now are we the sons of God, and it doth not yet appear what we shall be: but we know that, when he shall appear, we shall be like him; for we shall see him as he is. (1 John 3:1–2)

Precious in the sight of the Lord is the death of his saints. (Ps. 116:15)

For ye are dead, and your life is hid with Christ in God. When Christ, who is our life, shall appear, then shall ye also appear with him in glory. (Col. 3:3–4)

When death is nearing, will you be able to say with the apostle Paul:

I have fought a good fight, I have finished my course, I have kept the faith. (2 Tim. 4:7)

For we know that if our earthly house of this tabernacle were dissolved, we have a building of God, an house not made with hands, eternal in the heavens. (2 Cor. 5:1)

Beyond the Gate

Now the evening sun is sinking . . .
The day's hour is getting late.
Will the night with all its darkness
Find your soul outside the gate?

The ways to heaven are not many;
Its gate will open to but one.
Who has paid our fare to glory?
Jesus Christ, God's only Son!

Though we work from dawn to sundown,
Gaining riches, pomp, and fame,
We can only enter heaven
If we come in Jesus' name.

Of our lives God is the potter;
We are nothing but the clay.
Dust we are, to dust returning,
If we never seek God's way.

Yet, in mercy, still He is calling
To the wandering souls of men,
Who were born in sin and darkness,
And must yet be born again!

Jesus died for every sinner.
He can save each needy soul.
If you'll trust Him with your burden,
He will make your spirit whole!

Christ will give you peace and gladness
And remove your sin and doubt.
All who come in faith may enter;
Never one will be shut out!

Read each day the Holy Scriptures;
Soon with longing you will wait
For the Savior's welcome smile
And your home beyond the gate.

Then said Jesus unto them again, Verily, verily, I say unto
you, I am the door of the sheep. . . . I am the door: by me
if any man enter in, he shall be saved, and shall go in
and out, and find pasture. (John 10:7, 9)

Jesus answered and said unto him, Verily, verily, I say
unto thee, Except a man be born again, he cannot see
the kingdom of God. (John 3:3)

But we speak the wisdom of God in a mystery, even the
hidden wisdom, which God ordained before the world
unto our glory: . . . But as it is written, Eye hath not
seen, nor ear heard, neither have entered into the heart
of man, the things which God hath prepared for them
that love him. But God hath revealed them unto us by
his Spirit. (1 Cor. 2:7, 9–10a)

Winter Wonders

Hast thou entered into the treasures of the snow? (Job 38:22a)

No royal castle anywhere
In all the world would quite compare
To the glistening banks of pure white snow
That mount up high, as the north winds blow!
Each tiny flake is a jewel that shines
With perfection never found in mines!

Though trillions fall, each stands alone
In a feathery castle all its own.
As the moonlight shines
On that blanket of white,
A matchless wonder appears in sight!
With breathless splendor our eyes behold
A twinkling carpet, soft and cold.
Every hoarfrost sprinkled bush and tree
Forms a wonderland of mystery!

Our balsam hedge is bending low
'Neath a sparkling blanket of
New fallen snow!
Long stalagmites of ice,
Which the snowflakes form,
Drop by drop will vanish away.
Mother Nature says they cannot stay.

The winter sketch on my windowpane
Proves Jack Frost's brush has been busy again!

Behold! Through that window a face I spy
As I shovel the snow into piles high.

Soon the door bursts open and a little fellow,
Clad in snowsuit warm
And a scarf that's yellow,
With arms outstretched and face aglow,
Formed an angel in the snow!
As we rolled a snowball round and round,
A goose trail appeared on the frozen ground.
From that ball of snow a man we'd form
To reflect the beauty of the storm!

My dear child squealed and laughed with joy;
I had never seen a happier boy!
As I witnessed the thrill of my little lad,
How proud I was to be his dad,
And I thanked God, who reigns above
And forms each snowflake filled with love!

He giveth snow like wool: he scattereth the hoarfrost
like ashes. (Ps. 147:16)

My Best Birthday

Without merit, without power,
Without righteousness . . .
Without anything at all
My sinful soul to bless.
Without hope in this dark world;
Lost, alone, unwhole—
But God was not unmindful
Of the plight of my poor soul!
He sent a friend to tell me
Of His holy Word,
Because He knew I had a need
To know Christ as my Lord.

Though I'd never realized my sin,
God's words so strong and bright
Began to pierce my hardened heart
With a tiny ray of light.
And I began to think, *Oh my,*
What will I do when life is o'er
And it is time to die?
Then I read something in God's Book
About being born again,
That Jesus came and lived and died
To pay my debt of sin.
But Satan said, "Just do your best.
God surely wants no more;
The good works you can do, my friend,
Will land you on that shore!"

Each day I worked so hard for God
But had no inner peace;

Where could I turn and to whom go
From sin to get release?

Then in God's Word I heard one day
That Jesus is the door.
I came to Him and entered in,
Not fearful anymore!

So now I take some time each day
God's holy Word to read,
And I can do all things through Christ
Who has strength to meet my need!
Since I am anchored on the rock
And walk the narrow way,
I grow to love Him more and more
Every moment, every day!

Now I live to please my Savior,
Give Him all my future days.
He suffered so for my redemption,
And all He asks of me is praise!
I've had many happy birthdays
But never one as sweet
As that blessed, glorious day
When I knelt at Jesus' feet!

Not by *works* of righteousness which we have done, but according to his *mercy* he saved us, by the washing of regeneration, and renewing of the Holy Ghost; Which he shed on us abundantly through Jesus Christ our Saviour. (Titus 3:5–6 emphasis added)

His Cross

Jesus said, "Come bear your cross,
If you would follow Me.
The cross I bore, you need not take,
For I bore that, you see.
Just come to Me and seek My will;
Forsake your own for Mine;
I'll see your love and promise to
Be with you all the time!

"By grace, through faith,
God's perfect way . . . all men
May be redeemed today!
Go, spread the news, the marvelous news,
That men have been set free!

"Upon that cross I paid for sin,
But you must *believe* to enter in.
No longer can the law condemn.
So trust in Me; I am your friend!

"Hanging there between earth and sky,
I paid your debt. Why will ye die?
You cannot pay your debt of sin,
So come to Me and enter in!"

The apostle Paul, who so loved the Lord Jesus and suffered much in his name, desired to be "found in him, not having mine own righteousness, which is of the law, but that which is through the faith of Christ, the righteousness which is of God by *faith*" (Phil. 3:9 emphasis added).

Therefore being justified by faith, we have *peace* with God through our Lord Jesus Christ. (Rom. 5:1 emphasis added)

And he that taketh not his cross, and followeth after me, is not worthy of me. He that findeth his life shall lose it: and he that loseth his life for my sake shall find it. (Matt. 10:38–39)

Go ye therefore, and teach all nations, baptizing them in the name of the Father, and of the Son, and of the Holy Ghost. (Matt. 28:19)

Teaching them to observe all things whatsoever I have commanded you: and, lo, I am with you alway, even unto the end of the world. Amen. (Matt. 28:20)

For Christ is the end of the law for righteousness to every one that *believeth*. (Rom. 10:4 emphasis added)

So Christ was once offered to bear the sins of many; and unto them that look for him shall he appear the second time without sin unto salvation. (Heb. 9:28)

For Christ also hath once suffered for sins, the just for the unjust, that he might bring us to God, being put to death in the flesh, but quickened by the Spirit. (1 Pet. 3:18)

Whisper a Prayer

When the burdens of life seem too
Heavy to bear, hope will return
When you whisper a prayer!
Just trust and believe;
You will always be heard,
For God cannot lie and is true
To His Word.

When trouble and poverty knock at your door,
And your heart cries in anguish—
Oh, what could come more?
And sometimes you feel life isn't fair,
Just look to the Lord and whisper a prayer!

The grim reaper of death has entered your home,
And now you're left desolate, sad, and alone.
Take heart, weary pilgrim,
There is one who does care—
And hope will return when you whisper
A prayer!

If you've prayed many times and think
He's not heard, open God's Book,
And read in His Word.
When we ask in faith, He always will hear;
To Him every child is precious and dear!

So drop to your knees and trust
He *is* near to carry your burden
And banish your fear.
Though the burdens of life

Seem too heavy to bear,
Hope will return when you whisper a prayer!

O thou that hearest prayer, unto thee shall all flesh come.
(Ps. 65:2)

He will regard the prayer of the destitute, and not despise their prayer. (Ps. 102:17)

Confess your faults one to another, and pray one for another, that ye may be healed. The effectual fervent prayer of a righteous man availeth much. (James 5:16)

He that planted the ear, shall he not hear? he that formed the eye, shall he not see? (Ps. 94:9)

Looking Beyond

Looking beyond the cares of today,
Seeing horizons much farther away!
This life is a vapor, which soon will be past;
But new life through Jesus forever will last.
Looking beyond all pain and all tears
And seeing Christ's glory removes human fears.

Though clouds above are dark as night,
God's light of love is shining;
Truth is beyond the shadows—
There is a silver lining!

Just trust the Master Potter,
Who molds each piece of clay—
And when He is finished, rest assured,
We'll be perfect every way.

Remember, friend, to look beyond
Your cares and pain and tears;
Because the Lord has bought for you
Eternal, blessed years!

For he looked for a city which hath foundations, whose builder and maker is God. (Heb. 11:10)

There is a river, the streams whereof shall make glad the city of God, the holy place of the tabernacles of the most High. God is in the midst of her; she shall not be moved: God shall help her, and that right early. (Ps. 46:4–5)

But ye are come unto mount Sion, and unto the city of the living God, the heavenly Jerusalem, and to an innumerable company of angels, To the general assembly and church of the firstborn, which are written in heaven, and to God the Judge of all, and to the spirits of just men made perfect. (Heb. 12:22–23)

And the vessel that he made of clay was marred in the hand of the potter: so he made it again another vessel, as seemed good to the potter to make it. (Jer. 18:4)

I Will Rise Again

Oh, faithless children, tearful ones,
Whom seek ye at this tomb?
Why walk ye in such deep despair,
Heads bowed in fear and gloom?
Can't you remember what I spoke
When yet in Galilee?
I said, "I must be crucified
And hang upon a tree!"

Know ye not this simple truth?
When I have paid for sin,
No power on earth can keep Me bound;
I'll surely rise again!
For I am in My Father,
And My Father is in Me;
And victory I have won for you
Upon the cursed tree.

Can't you rejoice and just *believe*
That I have set you free?
Oh, open up your blinded eyes
And put your trust in Me.

Oh faithless children, tearful ones,
Whom seek ye at this tomb?
Why walk ye in such deep despair,
Heads bowed in fear and gloom?
Why? Think ye for a moment
That I would tell you lies?
Remember when I told you
On the third day I would rise?

Can't you now open up your heart
And let God's love shine in?
Can't you accept this truth—
My blood has paid for sin?
I go now to My Father's house,
Expecting you to pray.
Remembering always that I am
"The life, the truth, the way."

Him [Christ], being delivered by the determinate counsel and foreknowledge of God, ye have taken, and by wicked hands have crucified and slain: Whom God hath raised up, having loosed the pains of death: because it was not possible that he should be holden of it. (Acts 2:23–24)

For if we believe that Jesus died and rose again, even so them also which sleep in Jesus will God bring with him. (1 Thess. 4:14)

Jesus said unto her [Martha], I am the resurrection, and the life: he that *believeth* in me, though he were dead, yet shall he live: And whosoever liveth and *believeth* in me shall never die. Believest thou this? (John 11:25–26)

And God hath both raised up the Lord, and will also raise up us by his own power. (1 Cor. 6:14)

Thank You, Thank You

Thank You, thank You, gracious God,
For the precious holy blood
Of our Savior, Your dear Son—
Only beloved, begotten one.

Truly Father, Thou art love,
Sending to us from above . . .
The Son with whom You were
Well pleased, so man might have
Sin's burden eased!

Did I say eased? Not so, dear Lord,
For You have told us in Your Word,
As far as west is from the east,
Sins—from the greatest to the least—
Through that Lamb's blood
Are white as snow!
Complete forgiveness, men may know!

Thank You, thank You, gracious God,
For Your Son who shed His blood.
No other hope have we beside,
If we with Thee would e'er abide!

Unto thee, O God, do we give thanks, unto thee do we give thanks: for that thy name is near thy wondrous works declare. (Ps. 75:1)

Be it known unto you therefore, men and brethren, that through this man is preached unto you the forgiveness of sins: And by him all that *believe* are justified from all things, from which ye could not be justified by the law of Moses. (Acts 13:38–39)

As far as the east is from the west, so far hath he removed our transgressions from us. (Ps. 103:12)

Neither is there salvation in any other: for there is none other name under heaven given among men, whereby we must be saved. (Acts 4:12)

The Birthday Party

Pups are happy chewing bones,
But little boys like ice cream cones!
Pretzel sticks and lollipops
They dream about 'till Dad's car stops.

Dan's mom served as party favors
Colored cones in many flavors
Plus jelly beans and birthday cake!
The end result—a tummy ache.

Of course, you'd like to claim that you
Just ate too many barbeque!
And that lovely salad you didn't touch
Cannot relieve the problem much.

Besides, with all your stomach pain,
You're forced to run home in the rain!
That party looked so bright ahead,
But looking back you feel 'most dead.

I said in mine heart, Go to now, I will prove thee with mirth, therefore enjoy pleasure: and, behold, this also is vanity. (Eccl. 2:1)

Then I saw that wisdom excelleth folly, as far as light excelleth darkness. (Eccl. 2:13)

Heavenly Revelation

Oh, praise the Lord, the trump has blown!
And Christ returns to claim His own.
Hallelujah, what a day!
The tears of saints have fled away.
While angels hail His deity,
He shares a feast with you and me.

He clothed us all with garments of white;
Earth's fears and doubts have taken flight.
While eons pass and ages roll,
The love of God has filled each soul.
The worthy Lamb shall have our praise
As we honor Him through eternal days!

Gates of pearl, streets of gold,
Walls of jasper, gems untold!
But marvel of marvels, saints have seen the face
Of their redeemer King, who prepared this place.
He said, "I'll prepare a place for you;
That where I am, there ye may be too!"

There is no sun in this city foursquare,
Only pure light of His countenance there!
Through the Lamb's blood atonement
Each sin spot is healed.
All knowledge and wisdom in Christ are revealed.

But some family circles today have been broken,
For not all had heeded the word God had spoken.
God's solemn command in the Book for all time
Was, "Believe in My Son;
As the stars ye shall shine!"

Then shall the righteous shine forth as the sun in the kingdom of their Father. Who hath ears to hear, let him hear. (Matt. 13:43)

And they that be wise shall shine as the brightness of the firmament; and they that turn many to righteousness as the stars for ever and ever. (Dan. 12:3)

At the Office

Nell chews gum and makes it pop!
Ed thumps his foot and doesn't stop.
These flowers on the ledge near me
    Just irritate my allergy!
A hornet is buzzing 'round my desk,
But with love for insects I'm not blessed.
Boss comes in, doesn't shut the door—
All my finished sheets float to the floor.

It's a hot, hot day and the bubbler's hexed;
    Means a shot in the eye until
        It's fixed!
    They are passing the hat
        For a sick leave gift;
Guess Mac forgot he shouldn't lift.

The cleaning lady finished late;
    Thought the dust on my desk
        Would certainly wait!
Can't unlock my file; poor memory, you see.
That combination—was it nine or three?
    Wow! Got it open, lucky thing!
        Quick! Back to my desk;
        Hear that telephone ring?
Take an aspirin now; how my head aches.
When folks dial, must they make mistakes?

Buy chocolates, Sam. Don't munch
And crunch on peanut brittle after lunch.
And if I hear Fred's dentures clack
Just one more time, I'll blow my stack!

It just might rain; the sky looks
Gray. Forgot my umbrella again today.
Well, I'll catch a ride with one of the
Force; that is, if I finish on time, of course.
I am popular here; I really rate.
It's always my privilege to be working late!

Now the office is quiet; not a sound
Anywhere, only the noise of my squeaky chair.
Know what? I miss that office crew
In spite of annoying things they do.
I realize now I've not been fair;
How can they stand my squeaky chair?

He that saith he is in the light, and hateth his brother, is in darkness even until now. He that loveth his brother abideth in the light, and there is none occasion of stumbling in him. (1 John 2:9–10)

He that is slow to anger is better than the mighty; and he that ruleth his spirit than he that taketh a city. (Prov. 16:32)

Cease from anger, and forsake wrath: fret not thyself in any wise to do evil. (Ps. 37:8)

Wherefore, my beloved brethren, let every man be swift to hear, slow to speak, slow to wrath: For the wrath of man worketh not the righteousness of God. (James 1:19–20)

A New Year

Another year of time has flown,
And the trump of God has not yet blown,
Which proves our God is long-suffering still.
Not one
Shall perish against His will!

The Lord Himself shall soon descend,
Of sin and heartaches make an end.
The Babe who came so long ago
To Israel, the Christ of God, all men must know!

Herod sent men to Bethlehem;
Their search was diligent
'Till an unusual dream revealed to them
The wicked king's intent.
True worship was not his heart;
The child he would destroy.
So the wise men departed another way
As they worshiped with hearts of joy!

Wise men still sing of that holy birth
As the angels sang when He came to earth!
And for His return, true believers wait,
For we know He will come
And not be late.

The Lord is not slack concerning his promise, as some
men count slackness; but is longsuffering to us-ward,
not willing that any should perish, but that all should
come to repentance. (2 Pet. 3:9)

For if we sin willfully after that we have received the knowledge of the truth, there remaineth no more sacrifice for sins, but a certain fearful looking for of judgment and fiery indignation, which shall devour the adversaries. (Heb. 10:26–27)

Be glad in the Lord, and rejoice, ye righteous: and shout for joy, all ye that are upright in heart. (Ps. 32:11)

Hunter's Dilemma

Clean up rifle, find red cap.
Buy new jacket with a zip or snap.
Pay for license, two plus ten.
Hunting fever strikes again!

Put my warm boot linings in;
To forget them would be next to sin.
The agony of chilblained toes
Is a sure result of forgetting those!
Take deerskin mitts with liners too.
They'll revive my hands when they turn blue.

This year I plan to tag my own
And stay out of the party zone!
That party business is a mess;
You'll lose your friends to have success.

Maybe I'll shoot an eight-point buck . . .
Took my rabbit's foot along for luck!
Just can't think with rhyme or reason
When time gets close to hunting season.

I hope when it is time to go,
The precipitation will be snow.
It always gives me stomach pain
To set out hunting in the rain.

I pray it's not the same this year—
My heading home without a deer.
I'd rather hide 'most any place
Than head back home in such disgrace!

Let them shout for joy, and be glad, that favour my righteous cause: yea, let them say continually, Let the Lord be magnified, which hath pleasure in the prosperity of his servant. And my tongue shall speak of thy righteousness and of thy praise all the day long. (Ps. 35:27–28)

A Child Is Born

As shepherds watched their flocks that night,
Suddenly there came a light!
Brightly beaming from on high,
Illuminating earth and sky!

The Judean shepherds, their hearts
Filled with fright, fell on their faces
Before the bright light.
Then an angel appeared, saying, "Be not afraid!
Between God and men true peace has been made.
The child who sleepeth in Bethlehem's stall
Is the dear Son of God, the Savior of all!
Go now, see the Babe who in a manger lays."
The shepherds arose, and with hearts full
Of praise, they followed the star
That led to Bethlehem. There they worshiped
The Christ Child, the Savior of men!

On that holy night the Savior was sent
To fulfill all God's will, to make a new covenant.
Men need no more slay a blood sacrifice,
For the blood of this Lamb will always suffice.

In swaddling cloths that Babe did lie
Because "once for all" He was born to die.
Though by His own He was not received,
Multitudes on Him believed.
Believed it was for them He came;
Found peace and joy in Jesus' name!

Not ever before, or ever might be again . . .
Another gift given to redeem sinful men.

Take this gift of gifts; oh, accept Him today.
Just confess your need and to Him humbly pray.
Only then can you really rejoice in His birth
Or know His real purpose in coming to earth.

And we have seen and do testify that the Father sent the Son to be the Saviour of the world. (1 John 4:14)

He came unto his own, and his own received him not. But as many as received him, to them gave he power to become the sons of God, even to them that believe on his name. (John 1:11–12)

To him give all the prophets witness, that through his name whosoever believeth in him shall receive remission of sins. (Acts 10:43)

Childhood

Oh, to be a child again;
Life was always carefree then!

Although at times tears came, I know . . .
Like the time I broke my little toe,
Chasing brother in the yard
'Cause tagging him was oh, so hard.
Ted had longer legs than me;
He'd touch the goal and holler, "Free!"
Then I'd feel like a total freak,
When we were playing hide-and-seek.

Walking from school took hours in spring
'Cause sister and I'd pick flowers and sing!
There wasn't much that Mom could say
When we gave her our wild bouquet!
She told us God made everything—
Even the flowers that grow in spring.

Ted fed the rabbits while I fed the cat;
Then he'd run for his baseball bat!
And when the yard was no longer light,
Daddy would read 'till we kissed goodnight.
He told me how God loves me too
And would be with me the whole night through.

Oh, to be a child again;
Life was always carefree then!

Verily I say unto you, Whosoever shall not receive the
kingdom of God as a little child, he shall not enter

therein. And he took them up in his arms, put his hands upon them, and blessed them. (Mark 10:15–16)

Remember now thy Creator in the days of thy youth, while the evil days come not, nor the years draw nigh, when thou shalt say, I have no pleasure in them. (Eccl. 12:1)

The Pastor's Wife

Who is a towering pillar?
Who brightens up his life?
Who really cares and comforts?
It is the pastor's wife.

She'll not complain or fret
If things don't go her way;
But looking upward yet
Will fold her hands and pray!

She'll always faithful be,
Though days be drear or sunny,
And manages with wisdom
His household and his money!

Her ways reveal the Savior,
Who loves us without measure.
Her smile and gracious words
Each hour his heart will treasure.

His children call her "blessed"
And trust each wise decision,
As hour by hour and day by day
She guides their spiritual vision!

She is a towering pillar
Who brightens up his life.
Who else could care and comfort
Like the pastor's wife?

Therefore, brethren, we are debtors, not to the flesh, to live after the flesh. For if ye live after the flesh, ye shall die: but if ye through the Spirit do mortify the deeds of the body, ye shall live. For as many as are led by the Spirit of God, they are the sons of God. (Rom. 8:12–14)

Give Him Your Heart

This poem can be sung to the tune of "At Calvary," singing the last verse as the chorus.

Have you troubles that seem hard to bear?
There's a friend who knows your every care.
If today you come to Him in prayer,
He'll cleanse your heart.

Christ the Savior gave Himself for me.
Now from death and sin I am set free.
Yes, I know His wondrous love for me.
He won my heart!

Life is only but a few short years.
Soon in heaven God will dry our tears.
Like a father, when we call, He hears.
He knows our heart.

Troubles, heartaches, all will flee away.
Joy and peace will fill your heart today.
Jesus, like a shepherd, leads the way.
Give Him your heart!

O God, thou art my God; early will I seek thee: my soul thirsteth for thee, my flesh longeth for thee in a dry and thirsty land, where no water is; . . . My lips shall praise thee. . . . My soul shall be satisfied as with marrow and fatness; and my mouth shall praise thee with joyful lips. (Ps. 63:1, 3, 5)

Search me, O God, and know my heart: try me, and know my thoughts: And see if there be any wicked way in me, and lead me in the way everlasting. (Ps. 139:23–24)

Be ye also patient; establish your hearts: for the coming of the Lord draweth nigh. (James 5:8)

Busy Puppies

Puppies, as people,
Are busy each day
Whether loved by their masters
Or mongrels astray.

When pup isn't barking but still as a mouse,
A quick check reveals he's been eating his house!
His pink tongue is bleeding
From gnawing the door,
And sharp teeth have shredded
The rug on his floor.

One week ago Grandpa came—
And believe it, already
His slippers are transformed
To party confetti!

By day pup digs bone holes
All over the lawn;
At night hears the cock's crow
One hour before dawn.

In winter when snowflakes
Fall cold in the street,
He'll dash 'cross the carpet
With wet little feet!
Run helter and skelter,
With fur smooth as silk
And tail gaily wagging
While lapping up milk.

Butterflies scamper as he snaps
At their wings,
And bunnies must find holes;
Poor little things!

A toad is a plaything,
But pup 'most has fits.
One bite is enough; he drools and he spits!

Rover's soft head was made only to pet.
We love him and never have harmed him as yet.
Though he tries our patience,
We'll do him no harm,
For puppies are precious
Down on the farm!

And God said, Let the earth bring forth the living crea-
ture after his kind, cattle, and creeping thing, and beast
of the earth after his kind: and it was so. And God made
the beast of the earth after his kind, and cattle after their
kind, and every thing that creepeth upon the earth after
his kind: and God saw that it was good. (Gen. 1:24–25)

Duty or Privilege?

Do I long to win the wanderer
As he goes his weary way?
Or have I ever sadly said,
"My duty is to pray"?

As I tell a soul of Jesus
And the love He shed on me,
Do I see it as a duty
To set a sinner free?

As Christ is interceding
At the Father's throne above,
Is He counting it a duty . . .
Or doing it in love?

Lord, teach me to love the sinner,
Who by Satan yet is bound,
And consider it a privilege
That a lost one might be found!

Oh, let me ever glory in the cross
He bore for me,
And the privilege He gave me
To be His eternally!

Oh, to think that God would choose us
To do anything for Him,
Since we so often go astray
And are prone to fall in sin!

So let us with abounding joy
Send praises to the sky
And use each precious privilege
To serve Him 'till we die!

I am crucified with Christ: nevertheless I live; yet not I, but Christ liveth in me: and the life which I now live in the flesh I live by the faith of the Son of God, who loved me, and gave himself for me. (Gal. 2:20)

And as it is appointed unto men once to die, but after this the judgment. (Heb. 9:27)

The Risen Christ

Hallelujah! Christ is risen!
Friend, do you know what this means?
We may come into God's presence
Without penance, works, or schemes.
Now in heaven pleading for us
Is the Father's Son, our Lord.
He is risen as He promised
In the Scriptures, God's true Word!

Christ is risen! Hallelujah!
The Emmaus Road He walked,
And with those He loved so dearly,
He had fellowship and talked.
Though their eyes had not been opened
To reveal this friend so splendid,
Their hearts burned sore within them
As their saddened voices blended.

Hallelujah! Christ is risen!
How sweet Mary did rejoice.
When inquiring of the gardener,
She heard the Master's voice!
Hallelujah! Christ is risen!
See the angels at the tomb?
Rejoice! Rejoice! Disciples,
Banish thoughts of fear and gloom!

He has risen as He promised,
The first fruits of all who sleep;
Lives in heaven, interceding—
And each precious child will keep.

"Because I live, ye too shall live!"
Those joyous words He spoke!
Though some still doubt,
His words *were true;*
Don't take it as a joke.

God's power will provide
For His children a new body,
In resurrection glorified!
Now our bodies are terrestrial;
Then celestial they shall be
All because the blessed Savior
Rose again for you and me!
Oh, grave, where is thy victory?
Oh, death, where is thy sting?
Hallelujah! Hallelujah!
To our risen Lord, we sing.

He is not here, but is risen: remember how he spake
unto you when he was yet in Galilee, The Son of man
must be delivered into the hands of sinful men, and be
crucified, and the third day rise again. And they remem-
bered his words. (Luke 24:6–8)

Jesus saith unto her, Mary. She turned herself, and saith
unto him, Rabboni; which is to say, Master. (John 20:16)

Wherefore he is able also to save them to the uttermost
that come unto God by him, seeing he ever liveth to
make intercession for them. (Heb. 7:25)

For Christ is not entered into the holy places made with
hands, which are the figures of the true; but into heaven
itself, now to appear in the presence of God for us. (Heb.
9:24)

Victory

We praise Thee, God, for Thou art great,
Loving, good, and kind . . .
In mercy Thou hast sight renewed
To men who once were blind!

Compassion Thou wilt show to all
Who in Thy Son will trust.
If we would enter heaven's gate,
Believe in Him we must!

Great promises Thy Word has given
To help us on our way.
Strength and comfort, peace and joy
Will come to those who pray!

When earth's great darkness all has passed,
And heavenly dawn appears,
Our Savior's smile will well repay
All pain and toil and tears!

Old Satan, our great foe, is strong
Who gives to all sins' wages,
But faith the victory will take,
Though long the battle rages.

Within each child of God there dwells
Christ's overcoming power.
The Spirit of our living Lord
Brings victory for the hour!

When this frail life has passed away,
In heaven we'll plainly see
The blessing of our service here
All through eternity!

But now being made free from sin, and become servants
to God, ye have your fruit unto holiness, and the end
everlasting life. (Rom. 6:22)

The Lord is gracious, and full of compassion; slow to
anger, and of great mercy. (Ps. 145:8)

These things have I written unto you that *believe* on the
name of the Son of God; that ye may know that ye have
eternal life, and that ye may believe on the name of the
Son of God. (1 John 5:13)

Even as Abraham *believed* God, and it was accounted to
him for righteousness. Know ye therefore that they which
are of faith, the same are the children of Abraham. And
the scripture, foreseeing that God would justify the hea-
then [unbelieving] through faith, preached before the
gospel unto Abraham, saying, In thee shall all nations
be blessed. (Gal. 3:6–8)

For whatsoever is born of God overcometh the world:
and this is the victory that overcometh the world, even
our faith. Who is he that overcometh the world, but he
that *believeth* that Jesus is the Son of God? (1 John 5:4–
5)

You Care

Father, we thank You for
All of Your care.
We are glad we can call You
And know You are there!

Your grace is sufficient,
And this we believe so
Why don't we call more
And more grace receive?

In our hearts we desire
Your complete control;
For then we'll enjoy
Sweet peace in our soul!

Not only today do we thank
You in prayer, but ever and always
We will trust, for You care!

It is of the Lord's mercies that we are not consumed,
because his compassions fail not. (Lam. 3:22)

They are new every morning: great is thy faithfulness.
The Lord is my portion, saith my soul; therefore will I
hope in him. . . . It is good that a man should both hope
and quietly wait for the salvation of the Lord. (Lam. 3:22–
24, 26)

Seeing then that we have a great high priest, that is passed
into the heavens, Jesus the Son of God, let us hold fast
our profession. For we have not an high priest which

cannot be touched with the feeling of our infirmities; but was in all points tempted like as we are, yet without sin. Let us therefore come boldly unto the throne of grace, that we may obtain mercy, and find grace to help in time of need. (Heb. 4:14–16)

Friendship Seeds

Friendship is a garden
That awaits the tiny seeds
Of love and kindness,
Prayer and praise;
Followed by good deeds.

As these are found within our hearts,
And blossom in our life,
Our God will then be glorified;
And we'll ease our brother's strife!

God gave two lips to sing His praise,
Two hands to ease men's load;
He has a job for each of us
Who walk this earthly road.

So be a friend to someone
Who needs a friend indeed,
And let God plant within your heart
A tiny friendship seed!

First it will sprout,
Then it will grow
In the garden of your heart;
And others will be lifted up
Once friendship gets a start![3]

A friend loveth at all times, and a brother is born for adversity. (Prov. 17:17)

Ye are my friends, if ye do whatsoever I command you. Henceforth I call you not servants; for the servant knoweth not what his Lord doeth: but I have called you friends; for all things that I have heard of my Father I have made known unto you. (John 15:14–15)

Ye adulterers and adulteresses, know ye not that the friendship of the world is enmity with God? whosoever therefore will be a friend of the world is the enemy of God. (James 4:4)

Love One Another

Say, my brother, let me ask you—
If you couldn't get your way,
Could you still rejoice in Jesus,
Bow your head, and humbly pray?

Though your viewpoint may be different
Than your brother's in the Lord,
Will you trust the Lord to answer
All your questions through the Word?

Or do you stubbornly insist
That your way is always right?
And those who differ with your view
Are not walking in the light?
Can you bow your head before the Lord
And also bow your heart?
Or will you fight him to the death
Though it tear the church apart!

Now you say, "I am a leader,
And am sure God spoke to me!"
But He speaks to all the children
Who are in His family.

And the great command He gives us
Is to show love toward each other.
Lost men will see that we love God
When we love one another!

Most folk love those who love them too.
This is no noble deed;

But to love our enemies and seek their good
Will bring rich reward indeed!

Put on therefore, as the elect of God, holy and beloved, bowels of mercies, kindness, humbleness of mind, meekness, longsuffering; forbearing one another, and forgiving one another, if any man have a quarrel against any: even as Christ forgave you, so also do ye. And above all these things put on charity, which is the bond of perfectness. And let the peace of God rule in your hearts, to the which also ye are called in one body; and be ye thankful. (Col. 3:12–15)

These things I command you, that ye love one another. (John 15:17)

Depart from evil, and do good; seek peace, and pursue it. (Ps. 34:14)

Who art thou that judgest another man's servant? to his own master he standeth or falleth. Yea, he shall be holden up: for God is able to make him stand. (Rom. 14:4)

By this shall all men know that ye are my disciples, if ye have love one to another. (John 13:35)

But I say unto you which hear, Love your enemies, do good to them which hate you, bless them that curse you, and pray for them which despitefully use you. (Luke 6:27–28)

My little children, let us not love in word, neither in tongue; but in deed and in truth. (1 John 3:18)

The apostle Paul said to Philemon, "I thank my God, making mention of thee always in my prayers, hearing of thy love and faith, which thou hast toward the Lord Jesus, and toward all saints" (Philem. 1:4–5).

In a Manger Bed

Infant babes are born each day,
But few must sleep on a bed of hay.
Just think! The Christ Child had no bed;
No feathery spot to lay His head!
Most babes today have a lovely crib,
A warm layette, and a character bib.

Mary placed her babe in a manger bed,
As years before, the prophets had said!
She gently wrapped Him in swaddling
Cloths. These were used for burials
Along with spices and cloves.

As we ponder this and wonder why,
The answer comes, "He was born to die."
Isaiah, the prophet, said a child would
Arrive, who would die for sin,
Making many alive!

No room in the inn to lay His head,
But He slept, content in the manger bed!
While around the manger, glory and honor
Were bestowed on the child,
Son of God, the Father!

He healed the sick and raised the dead;
That babe who came to the manger bed.
Amazing miracle! What a unique thing,
That humble child was born a king!

God's gift of life for every nation.
So come, my friend, and receive Savior.
Then worship Him in adoration!

All that the Father giveth me shall come to me; and him that cometh to me I will in no wise cast out. (John 6:37)

Dayspring from on high hath visited us, to give light to them that sit in darkness and in the shadow of death, to guide our feet into the way of peace. (Luke 1:78b–79)

Therefore the Lord himself shall give you a sign; Behold, a virgin shall conceive, and bear a son, and shall call his name Immanuel. (Isa. 7:14)

For the grace of God that bringeth salvation hath appeared to all men. (Titus 2:11)

For God so loved the world, that he gave his only begotten Son, that whosoever *believeth* in him should not perish, but have everlasting life. (John 3:16 emphasis added)

Verily, verily, I say unto you, He that heareth my word, and believeth on him that sent me, hath everlasting life, and shall not come into condemnation; but is passed from death unto life. (John 5:24)

Grace

Since the Christ from death arose,
He is victor of our foes.
Faith that lets this Savior in
Frees the soul from death and sin!

Naught can separate that one
Who has trusted in God's Son
From the love of God, whose grace
Gives to all a hiding place!

And a man shall be as an hiding place from the wind,
and a covert from the tempest; as rivers of water in a dry
place, as the shadow of a great rock in a weary land!
(Isa. 32:2)

Though we tremble in the storm,
He will keep us safe and warm.
Safe beneath God's sheltering wing,
Day by day His praise to sing!

Oh, may we ever trust the Lord,
And find sweet peace within His Word.
Not asking Him the reason why,
But trusting, since He cannot lie.

God is not a man that he should lie; neither the son of
man, that he should repent; hath he said, and shall he
not do it? Hath he spoken and shall he not make it good?
(Num. 23:19)

God, by faith, Christ will reveal;
Believers with His Spirit seal!
Thus His kingdom they inherit;
All through grace, not works or merit.

Millions yet are Satan's slaves,
Perishing in Christless graves.
Oh, dear Savior, may they see
The light of love shine out through me!

Let me all of self forsake, that
I may this message take.
How that Christ from death arose
And has conquered all men's foes!

Faith in Christ the Son of God,
Who for man's sins shed His blood,
Brings freedom from the devil's power
And victory in death's trying hour.

Forasmuch as ye know that ye were not redeemed with
corruptible things, as silver and gold, from your vain
conversation received by tradition from your fathers; but
with the precious blood of Christ, as of a lamb without
blemish and without spot: Who verily was foreordained
before the foundation of the world, but was manifest in
these last times for you. (1 Pet. 1:18–20a)

Men without Christ now must know,
They, through Him, to heaven may go,
Since there is but one resting place,
And that is in God's arms of grace!

I am he that liveth, and was dead; and, behold, I am
alive for evermore, Amen; and have the keys of hell and
of death. (Rev. 1:18)

For sin shall not have dominion over you: for ye are not
under the law, but under grace. What then? shall we
sin, because we are not under the law, but under grace?
God forbid. Know ye not, that to whom ye yield your-
selves servants to obey, his servants ye are to whom ye
obey; whether of sin unto death, or of obedience unto
righteousness? (Rom. 6:14–16)

And they said, Believe on the Lord Jesus Christ, and thou
shalt be saved, and thy house. (Acts 16:31)

That if thou shalt confess with thy mouth the Lord Jesus,
and shalt believe in thine heart that God hath raised him
from the dead, thou shalt be saved. For with the heart
man believeth unto righteousness; and with the mouth
confession is made unto salvation. (Rom. 10:9–10)

For the righteous Lord loveth righteousness; his coun-
tenance doth behold the upright. (Ps. 11:7)

Keep me as the apple of the eye, hide me under the
shadow of thy wings. (Ps. 17:8)

For God sent not his Son into the world to condemn the
world; but that the world through him might be saved.
(John 3:17)

For by grace are ye saved through faith; and that not of
yourselves: it is the gift of God: Not of works, lest any
man should boast. (Eph. 2:8–9)

Not by works of righteousness which we have done, but
according to his mercy he saved us, by the washing of

regeneration, and renewing of the Holy Ghost; which he shed on us abundantly through Jesus Christ our Saviour; that being justified by his grace, we should be made heirs according to the hope of eternal life. (Titus 3:5–7)

Having therefore, brethren, boldness to enter into the holiest by the blood of Jesus, by a new and living way, which he hath consecrated for us, through the veil, that is to say, his flesh; and having an high priest over the house of God. (Heb. 10:19–21)

The eternal God is thy refuge, and underneath are the everlasting arms: and he shall thrust out the enemy from before thee; and shall say, Destroy them. (Deut. 33:27)

Come unto me, all ye that labour and are heavy laden, and I will give you rest. Take my yoke upon you, and learn of me; for I am meek and lowly in heart: and ye shall find rest unto your souls. (Matt. 11:28–29)

An Enchanting Rose

Neither novel, poetry, or prose
Can stir the soul as a perfect rose!
Velvet dew-dropped petals
Majestically unfold,
Revealing a scarlet beauty
For the clouds to behold!

A soft summer breeze wafts an exotic scent
Until hurricane winds, destruction bent,
Send velvet petals sailing through the air,
Spreading perfume everywhere!

Yet branch and leaf show no concern,
While bud after bud with smiling face
Appear from nowhere to take its place.

A sassy hummingbird flits gaily along,
Humming his carefree traveler's song.
Some busy, hard-working honeybees
Detect a fragrance in the breeze,
Then scramble nimbly from bud to rose
While nourishing nectar
In their honeycomb grows!

But day follows night, and night follows day,
'Till at last every petal has blown away.
Oh mystery! Sweet mystery!
That barren bush will produce again
Through dormant life entrapped within.

The grass withereth, the flower fadeth: but the word of our God shall stand for ever. (Isa. 40:8)

And so it is written, The first man Adam was made a living soul; the last Adam was made a quickening spirit. (1 Cor. 15:45)

And as we have borne the image of the earthy, we shall also bear the image of the heavenly. (1 Cor. 15:49)

But if the Spirit of him that raised up Jesus from the dead dwell in you, he that raised up Christ from the dead shall also quicken your mortal bodies by his Spirit that dwelleth in you. (Rom. 8:11)

He that hath the Son hath life; and he that hath not the Son of God hath not life. (1 John 5:12)

And the Lord God formed man of the dust of the ground, and breathed into his nostrils the breath of life; and man became a living soul. (Gen. 2:7)

Thank You, God

Thank You, God, for another day,
And thanks for listening when I pray!
Thanks for blessings from Your hand,
For promises that will ever stand.

For salvation that Your love has given,
Your presence now, and a home in heaven.
Thanks for Jesus, who bore the cross,
Counting earthly gain but loss.

Was ever a gift so costly given
As the Son of God, our gift from heaven?
Thank You, Lord, for home and friends,
For eternity that never ends!

For the sun that sets in breathless splendor
To rise again o'er the hills up yonder.
Thanks, dear Lord, for air and water;
For parents dear, and son and daughter.

For flickering flames on our fireside hearth;
A time for work and a time for mirth!
Thank You, God, for the simple things
And the privileges each new day brings.

Thanks for stars in the dark night sky
And the distant sound of a night owl's cry.
Yes, thank You, Lord, for each bright new day,
And thanks for listening when I pray!

The sacrifice of the wicked is an abomination to the Lord: but the prayer of the upright is his delight. (Prov. 15:8)

Offer unto God thanksgiving; and pay thy vows unto the most High. (Ps. 50:14)

Blessed be God, which hath not turned away my prayer, nor his mercy from me. (Ps. 66:20)

Rejoice in the Lord, O ye righteous: for praise is comely for the upright. (Ps. 33:1)

I will praise the name of God with a song, and will magnify him with thanksgiving. (Ps. 69:30)

Ye are blessed of the Lord which made heaven and earth. The heaven, even the heavens, are the Lord's: but the earth hath he given to the children of men. (Ps. 115:15–16)

It is a good thing to give thanks unto the Lord, and to sing praises unto thy name, O most High. (Ps. 92:1)

And whatsoever ye do in word or deed, do all in the name of the Lord Jesus, giving thanks to God and the Father by him. (Col. 3:17)

Picnic Joys?

A fly in my lemonade
And ants in my cake.
I hiked through the willows
And met up with a snake!

Went for a swimming dip,
Tripped on a stone.
Result of the water temp—
Chilled to the bone!

Laid in the sunshine,
Expecting a tan;
Now feel like a lobster
Fried in a pan!

Thirsty as a camel,
But the picnic jug is warm.
Billowing clouds above me
Push an upcoming storm!

My paper plate is sailing
Over stumps and swings—
So much for the joys
A summer picnic brings!

Rejoice in the Lord alway: and again I say, Rejoice. (Phil. 4:4)

Yet I will rejoice in the Lord, I will joy in the God of my salvation. (Hab. 3:18)

Go to the ant, thou sluggard; consider her ways, and be wise: Which having no guide, overseer, or ruler, provideth her meat in the summer, and gathereth her food in the harvest. (Prov. 6:6–8)

Now the serpent was more subtle than any beast of the field which the Lord God had made. And he said unto the woman, Yea, hath God said, Ye shall not eat of every tree of the garden? (Gen. 3:1)

And he tempted Eve to disobey God in the Garden of Eden, which caused the original sin of disobedience to be passed upon all men.

I Will Trust

Sometimes I ask, Lord, why
Should this test be in my life?
Why must I weep and suffer
With this heartache and this strife?
And yet I know my heavenly Father,
Will never, ever send
A thing to hurt this child of His,
Because He is my friend!

So I will not be discouraged,
For tomorrow I will know
Why the Lord allowed to come
Some things that hurt me so.
Then I will sing His praises
For the wisdom of His love;
And His mercy, oh, so precious—
Yes, I will know it all above!

So I'll trust in His good purpose
Because His Word is true;
And one day He'll explain it all,
Away beyond the blue!
I am very, very sure
God knows my need and cares;
And in His love He comforts me,
Through faith and through your prayers!

Thus saith the Lord; cursed be the man that trusteth in man, and maketh flesh his arm, and whose heart departeth from the Lord. . . . Blessed is the man that trusteth in the Lord, and whose hope the Lord is. (Jer. 17:5, 7)

The name of the Lord is a strong tower: the righteous runneth into it, and is safe. (Prov. 18:10)

Knowing this, that the trying of your faith worketh patience. But let patience have her perfect work, that ye may be perfect and entire, wanting nothing. (James 1:3–4)

That the trial of your faith, being much more precious than of gold that perisheth, though it be tried with fire, might be found unto praise and honour and glory at the appearing of Jesus Christ. (1 Pet. 1:7)

It is better to trust in the Lord than to put confidence in man. It is better to trust in the Lord than to put confidence in princes. (Ps. 118:8–9)

And unto man he said, Behold, the fear of the Lord, that is wisdom; and to depart from evil is understanding. (Job 28:28)

Serve the Lord with fear, and rejoice with trembling. Kiss the Son, lest he be angry, and ye perish from the way, when his wrath is kindled but a little. Blessed are all they that put their trust in him. (Ps. 2:11–12)

While it is said, *Today* if ye will hear his voice, harden not your hearts, as in the provocation. . . . For some, when they had heard, did provoke: howbeit not all that came out of Egypt by Moses. And to whom sware he that they should not enter into his rest, but to them that believed not? So we see that they could not enter in because of *unbelief*. (Heb. 3:15, 18–19 emphasis added)

The Lord is nigh unto all them that call upon him, to all that call upon him in truth. (Ps. 145:18)

Slowing Down?

Do you feel that you are slowing down,
Losing all your zest?
Often wishing you could stop
And take a little rest?

Well, that's your privilege, my friend.
Down through the years you've earned it!
And aren't you glad you read God's Book
While many others spurned it?

There are so many promises
Hidden in God's Word,
And the very best of all
Says we'll be with the Lord!

The hoary head is a crown of glory, if it be found in the way of righteousness. (Prov. 16:31)

Let not your heart be troubled: ye believe in God, believe also in me. In my Father's house are many mansions: if it were not so, I would have told you. I go to prepare a place for you. And if I go and prepare a place for you, I will come again, and receive you unto myself; that where I am, there ye may be also. (John 14:1–3)

Blessings are upon the head of the just: but violence covereth the mouth of the wicked. (Prov. 10:6)

The memory of the just is blessed. (Prov. 10:7a)

Therefore the redeemed of the Lord shall return, and come with singing unto Zion; and everlasting joy shall be upon their head: they shall obtain gladness and joy; and sorrow and mourning shall flee away. (Isa. 51:11)

Is God Real?

Yes, friend, there is a God—just *one,*
Who, in the person of His Son,
Paid sin's debt for everyone!
If there were no God, man could not exist;
Through His might and power
All things consist!

Man was naught but dust until
God's breath of power gave him life!
Then Satan tempted Eve, his wife,
And they both fell to heartache and strife!

Briars and thistles sprang forth from the earth.
While Adam and Eve now needed rebirth.
And all generations mankind since then
Can only reach God through repentance of sin!

But when God's only Son ascended to heaven,
The Spirit of God to all men was given!
Yet, only through faith, this gift we obtain.
So trust in God's Son
Who for your sin was slain.
God's grace is a mystery man can't comprehend,
But through faith He will keep us unto the end!

Now unto him that is able to keep you from falling, and
to present you faultless before the presence of his glory
with exceeding joy, to the only wise God our Saviour, be
glory and majesty, dominion and power, both now and
for ever. Amen. (Jude 24–25)

God is real! God is all powerful! And He is ever present!

Always remember that "many deceivers are entered into the world, who confess not that Jesus Christ is come in the flesh. This is a deceiver and an antichrist" (2 John 1:7).

God's Word says that Christ

> "is the image of the invisible God, the firstborn of every creature: For by him were all things created, that are in heaven, and that are in earth, visible and invisible, whether they be thrones, or dominions, or principalities, or powers: all things were created by him, and for him: And he is before all things, and by him all things consist. . . . For it pleased the Father that in him should all fullness dwell. (Col. 1:15–17, 19)

> If we confess our sins, he is faithful and just to forgive us our sins, and to cleanse us from all unrighteousness. (1 John 1:9)

> All that the Father giveth me shall come to me; and him that cometh to me I will in no wise cast out. (John 6:37)

> Not by works of righteousness which we have done, but according to his *mercy* he saved us, by the washing of regeneration, and renewing of the Holy Ghost; which he shed on us abundantly through Jesus Christ our Saviour. (Titus 3:5–6)

Is there a question in your heart? Why would God love man enough to allow his Son to die on the cross for us? For the same reason that He loved the Israelites!

The Conquest of the Promised Land

Old Balaam rode a donkey
Which he in anger smote,
Then was amazed when hearing
Words coming from his throat!
It seemed that little donkey
Had more sense than he,
For Balaam, in rebellion,
The angel couldn't see!

The jealousy of Korah
Was very, very great.
For Moses and for Aaron,
His heart held only hate.

To be so very jealous
In God's sight is a sin.
Do you remember how the earth
Took Korah and his friends in?

When no water could be found,
The Israelites complained.
As Moses heard them murmur,
His heart was greatly pained.

In anger he did strike the rock,
And water from it poured!
God gives us living water
When we trust Christ as Lord!

We learned about a serpent
Moses hung upon a pole

To take away the sting of death
And make the people whole.
Jesus hung upon the cross
To take away our sin.
He will forgive when we believe,
And heaven we'll enter in!

While in the land of Moab,
The prophet Moses died,
So then another leader,
Named Joshua, God supplied.

God's children have a leader,
Who is ever by their side.
If you have trusted Jesus,
He wants to be your guide!

Under flax stalks on a rooftop,
Rahab hid two spies one day,
Then trusting in the red cord,
Stole her kinfolks safe away!

As the priests' feet touched the water,
The Jordan became dry ground!
So people and ark passed over,
Quite safely, we have found.

The walls of Jericho, great and high,
God caused to tumble down
Because the people did obey
And compassed it around!

We know that Achan was a thief,
And for his sin he died.

Perhaps sometime you've stolen
And to the Lord have cried,
"Oh, Jesus, how I thank You,
That for my sin You died!"

If we believe that God is great,
And seek His holy will,
He can do miracles, we are told.
He made the sun stand still!

Now Caleb was a man with
Courage beyond measure.
Through trusting God
He gained the land of Hebron
For his treasure.

As we study all the Scripture
And then obey it too,
The Lord will surely guide our steps
Each day our whole life through.

If we will trust Christ every day
We'll find that He is with us.
The Bible says that He will *never*
Leave us nor forsake us!

But the angel of the Lord stood in a path of the vine-
yards, a wall being on this side, and a wall on that side.
And when the ass saw the angel of the Lord, she thrust
herself unto the wall, and crushed Balaam's foot against
the wall: and he smote her again. . . . And the Lord opened
the mouth of the ass, and she said unto Balaam, What
have I done unto thee, that thou hast smitten me these
three times? . . . And the angel of the Lord said unto

him, Wherefore hast thou smitten thine ass these three times? behold, I went out to withstand thee, because thy way is perverse before me: . . . And Balaam said unto the angel of the Lord, I have sinned; for I knew not that thou stoodest in the way against me: now therefore, if it displease thee, I will get me back again. (Num. 22:24–25, 28, 32, 34)

And Moses lifted up his hand, and with his rod he smote the rock twice: and the water came out abundantly, and the congregation drank, and their beasts also. (Num. 20:11)

And Moses made a serpent of brass, and put it upon a pole, and it came to pass, that if a serpent had bitten any man, when he beheld the serpent of brass, he lived. (Num. 21:9)

Behold, when we come into the land, thou shalt bind this line of scarlet thread in the window which thou didst let us down by: and thou shalt bring thy father, and thy mother, and thy brethren, and all thy father's household, home unto thee. (Josh. 2:18)

And the priests that bare the ark of the covenant of the Lord stood firm on dry ground in the midst of Jordan, and all the Israelites passed over on dry ground, until all the people were passed clean over Jordan. (Josh. 3:17)

So the people shouted when the priests blew with the trumpets: and it came to pass, when the people heard the sound of the trumpet, and the people shouted with a great shout, that the wall fell down flat, so that the people went up into the city, every man straight before him, and they took the city. (Josh. 6:20)

The Twilight Hour

Hark! What great anticipation
Doth the twilight hour bring.
As the lark before the sunrise,
So my heart begins to sing!

For so long my soul has waited,
And so oft my lips have prayed
For the coming of the Master
In His kingly robes arrayed!

Rejoice! Rejoice! Oh, Christian,
As the shades of evening lower
And the moment fast approacheth
When our Lord shall come in power.

Faith has gained for us the victory
And has banished every fear.
Now eternal day is dawning;
Soon God's trumpet we will hear!

Then all trouble will be over,
When we reach the heavenly shore.
Though now, passing through the twilight;
There, all tears shall fall no more.

Let the redeemed rejoice and praise God
As they fall upon their knees,
For in heaven Christ still liveth
And returneth when He please.

While the world in darkness flounders,
And "God is dead!" man cries,

Faith looks up and knows full well
Jehovah never dies.

Every precious promise Christ has given
Must endure, and His bride,
Who fully trusts Him,
In His Word may rest secure!

In the valley of decision
Stand great multitudes of men
Who have never known that Jesus said,
"Ye *must* be born again."

Let us pray the Holy Spirit
Will convict them with great power
And lead them to the Savior now
In this the twilight hour!
Since the heavenly Groom soon cometh,
Let His earthly bride prepare,
Through His grace, herself adorning
With His righteous robe so fair!

Lo! How fast the twilight passes
As she thinks upon tomorrow.
Happy thoughts about the wedding
Quickly banish every sorrow!

The evening now has darkened;
Lengthy shadows fill the room,
But the bride seems not to notice
For her mind is on the groom!

Days of work and preparation
Never tire her the least

As she thinks about her lover
And the coming wedding feast!

Hark! What great anticipation
Doth the twilight hour bring.
As the lark before the sunrise,
So her heart begins to sing!

In the valley of the shadows
Christ awaits the church, His bride,
While the blessed Holy Spirit
Leads her safely to His side.

They shall never more be parted
By earth's rough and stormy weather,
But so happily united,
Dwell eternally together!

Hark! What great anticipation
Doth the twilight hour bring
To the church and to the Savior,
Who shall reign as righteous King.

I know that, whatsoever God doeth, it shall be *for ever:*
nothing can be put to it, nor any thing taken from it:
and God *doeth it,* that men should fear before him. (Eccl.
3:14 emphasis added)

It is a fearful thing to fall into the hands of the living
God. (Heb. 10:31)

Oh that men would realize that God is God, and that His
Word *will* come to pass! Jesus said:

"For verily I say unto you, Till heaven and earth pass, one jot or one tittle shall in no wise pass from the law, till all be fulfilled" (Matt. 5:18).

Christ fulfilled the law for us, by His sinless life and atoning death!

Multitudes, multitudes in the valley of decision: for the day of the Lord is near in the valley of decision. (Joel 3:14)

The fruit of the righteous is a tree of life; and he that winneth souls is wise. (Prov. 11:30)

In the way of righteousness is life; and in the pathway thereof there is no death. (Prov. 12:28)

He, that being often reproved hardeneth his neck, shall suddenly be destroyed, and that without remedy. (Prov. 29:1)

For the Lord himself shall descend from heaven with a shout, with the voice of the archangel, and with the trump of God: and the dead in Christ shall rise first: Then we which are alive and remain shall be caught up together with them in the clouds, to meet the Lord in the air: and so shall we ever be with the Lord. Wherefore comfort one another with these words. (1 Thess. 4:16–18)

Even so, come, Lord Jesus! (Rev. 22:20)

Seek ye the Lord while he may be found, call ye upon him while he is near: Let the wicked forsake his way, and the unrighteous man his thoughts: and let him return unto the Lord, and he *will* have mercy upon him; and to our God, for he will *abundantly pardon*. (Isa. 55:6–7 emphasis added)

Right Where You Are

Would you win lost souls to Christ
On some mission field afar?
Then you must begin today
In the place right where you are!
Broken hearts need mending;
But wherever came the notion
That those who need the Savior most
Live far across the ocean?

Perhaps someone right next to you
Has a sad and aching heart
And feels so lonely every day.
Right now, please do your part!
The time to love for Jesus' sake
Is not in future years.
Now is God's accepted time
To dry another's tears!

So show a loving spirit
To a lonely soul in need,
And help a wandering sheep
Into God's fold to feed.
No promise for tomorrow
Or a wish upon a star
Will bring more joy to Jesus
Than to serve right where you are!

Perhaps someone right in your home
Must see how kind you are,
For caring must begin right now
If we would serve afar!

Yes, folks around us everywhere
Are longing for some love,
Then they will put their faith in Christ
Who lives for them above.

Could be a desperate, unhappy soul
Is near enough to touch,
And dreams of future service
Won't help that sad heart much.
If we would win lost souls to Christ
On some mission field afar,
Then let us serve the Lord today
In the place right where we are!

Our goal must be to show Christ's love
As to God's will we yield;
When we obey, then we will reap
In God's ripe harvest field!

. . . Look on the fields; for they are white already to harvest. (John 4:35b)

. . . Behold, now is the accepted time; behold, now is the day of salvation. (2 Cor. 6:2b)

He that goeth forth and weepeth, bearing precious seed, shall doubtless come again with rejoicing, bringing his sheaves with him. (Ps. 126:6)

Therefore to him that knoweth to do good, and doeth it not, to him it is sin. (James 4:17)

We love him, because he first loved us. (1 John 4:19)

Year's End

My calendar shows December,
And time is on the run!
E're just a few more days have passed
Another year is done.
How time can pass so swiftly
Is hard to understand.
As I recall, I haven't finished
Half the things I'd planned.

Last New Year's Eve I was convinced
I'd keep my resolutions.
Thought all life's problems coming up
Would have positive solutions!

Somehow that has not been the case,
And I'm mighty glad to know
There is another year ahead
In which to live and grow!

So I'll just walk on day by day,
Trusting God to lead.
Because I know He plans my way,
I will have peace indeed!

Blessed be the name of the Lord from this time forth and
for evermore. (Ps. 113:2)

A land which the Lord thy God careth for: the eyes of
the Lord thy God are always upon it, from the begin-
ning of the year even unto the end of the year. (Deut.
11:12)

And, Thou, Lord, in the beginning hast laid the foundation of the earth; and the heavens are the works of thine hands: They shall perish; but thou remainest; and they all shall wax old as doth a garment; And as a vesture shalt thou fold them up, and they shall be changed: but thou art the same, and thy years shall not fail. (Heb. 1:10–12)

Thou turnest man to destruction; and sayest, Return, ye children of men. For a thousand years in thy sight are but as yesterday when it is past, and as a watch in the night. (Ps. 90:3–4)

And therefore will the Lord wait, that he may be gracious unto you, and therefore will he be exalted, that he may have mercy upon you: for the Lord is a God of judgment: blessed are all they that wait for him. (Isa. 30:18)

And the times of this ignorance God winked at; but now commandeth all men every where to repent: Because he hath appointed a day, in the which he will judge the world in righteousness by that man whom he hath ordained; whereof he hath given assurance unto all men, in that he hath raised him from the dead. (Acts 17:30–31)

Time

"Tell me, dear, when must we leave?
What time should we arrive?
Oh, my! You say it's four fifteen?
I understood it was five!"

It's six A.M. The sun is up,
And time to head for work.
Must get the kids awake for school,
Lest they their duties shirk!

We often think of daughter, Ann,
Expecting baby five,
And always wonder just what time
That bundle will arrive.
Today could be the very day
A new life will be born
While yet another soul may leave
Loved ones and friends forlorn.

The snow is gone; it's springtime now
And time to sow some seeds
In our little garden,
Then time to watch for weeds!

Summertime is almost here
With flowers, birds, and bees.
Our robin is back and starts his nest
High in our lilac trees!

Picnic time and time to swim;
Time for tennis and golf,
But mother says, "It's canning time.

Time to put fruits on the shelf!"
Johnny says, "It's camping time."

And "vacation time," said Sue—
But who takes time to stop and ask,
"God, what would You have me do?"
Since time is very precious,
We must be wise and learn
That moments lost to Satan
Never will return!

The Holy Scriptures teach us
That when this time is o'er,
We shall be with Jesus
And time shall be no more.

So let us number our days that we may apply our hearts unto wisdom. (Ps. 90:12)

Here have we no continuing city, but we seek one to come. (Heb. 13:14)

To everything there is a season, and a time to every purpose under heaven. (Eccl. 3:1)

Knowing the time, now it is high time to awake out of sleep. (Rom. 13:11a)

Awake thou that sleepest and arise from the dead, and Christ shall give thee light. (Eph. 5:14)

A time to be born and a time to die, a time to plant and a time to pluck up that which is planted. (Eccl. 3:2)

Waiting Still

Time is still with us—
It is still called today,
And the Savior still waiting
For sinners to pray!
His love will not fail us;
It abounds without measure—
And He longs to forgive you.
Yes, this is His pleasure!

So, friend, why not hasten
To kneel at the cross?
Say goodbye forever to sin
And its cost.

You will find joy and peace
As you walk in His will,
So do come *today*
While He is waiting still!

Have you come to Christ with your burden of sin and asked His forgiveness?

Though you may have doubts, remember that Christ distinguished between doubt and unbelief. Doubt is can't believe; unbelief is won't believe. Doubt is honesty, unbelief is obstinacy. Doubt is looking for light; unbelief is content with darkness.

—Henry Drummond

Thou Lord, art good, and ready to forgive, and plenteous in *mercy* unto *all* them that *call* upon thee. (Ps. 86:5 emphasis added)

> Have I any pleasure at all that the wicked should die? saith the Lord God: and not that he should return from his ways, and live? (Ezek. 18:23)

Why is He still waiting, friend? Because God is *love*. He "is longsuffering to us-ward, not willing that any should perish, but that all should come to repentance" (2 Pet. 3:9).

> For if the word spoken by angels was steadfast, and every transgression and disobedience received a just recompense of reward; how shall we escape, if we neglect so great salvation; which at the first began to be spoken by the Lord, and was confirmed unto us by them that heard him; God also bearing them witness, both with signs and wonders, and with divers miracles, and gifts of the Holy Ghost, according to his own will? (Heb. 2:2–4)

> And the ransomed of the Lord shall return, and come to Zion with songs and everlasting joy upon their heads: they shall obtain joy and gladness, and sorrow and sighing shall flee away. (Isa. 35:10)

> But the day of the Lord *will come* as a thief in the night; in the which the heavens shall pass away with a great noise, and the elements shall melt with fervent heat, the earth also and the works that are therein shall be burned up. (2 Pet. 3:10 emphasis added)

> And this know, that if the goodman of the house had known what hour the thief would come, he would have watched, and not have suffered his house to be broken through. Be ye therefore ready also: for the Son of man cometh at an hour when ye think not. (Luke 12:39–40)

Index

To order additional copies of

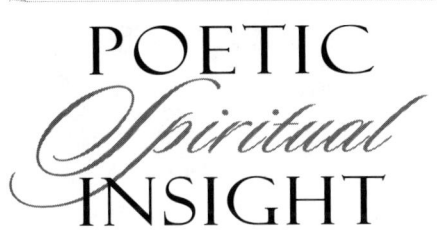

POETIC

Spiritual

INSIGHT

Have your credit card ready and call

Toll free: (877) 421-READ (7323)

or send $9.95* each plus $4.95 S&H**

to
WinePress Publishing
PO Box 428
Enumclaw, WA 98022

*Washington residents please add 8.4% tax.
**Add $1.50 S&H for each additional book ordered.